Security Tokens and Stablecoins Quick Start Guide

Learn how to build STO and stablecoin decentralized applications

Weimin Sun
Xun (Brian) Wu
Angela Kwok

BIRMINGHAM - MUMBAI

Security Tokens and Stablecoins Quick Start Guide

Commissioning Editor: Sunith Shetty
Acquisition Editor: Joshua Nadar
Content Development Editor: Pratik Andrade, Anugraha Arunagiri
Technical Editor: Jovita Alva
Copy Editor: Safis Editing
Project Coordinator: Namrata Swetta
Proofreader: Safis Editing
Indexer: Rekha Nair
Graphics: Jisha Chirayil
Production Coordinator: Shraddha Falebhai

First published: April 2019

Production reference: 1300419

Published by Packt Publishing Ltd.
Livery Place
35 Livery Street
Birmingham
B3 2PB, UK.

ISBN 978-1-83855-106-3

www.packtpub.com

`mapt.io`

Mapt is an online digital library that gives you full access to over 5,000 books and videos, as well as industry leading tools to help you plan your personal development and advance your career. For more information, please visit our website.

Why subscribe?

- Spend less time learning and more time coding with practical eBooks and Videos from over 4,000 industry professionals

- Improve your learning with Skill Plans built especially for you

- Get a free eBook or video every month

- Mapt is fully searchable

- Copy and paste, print, and bookmark content

Packt.com

Did you know that Packt offers eBook versions of every book published, with PDF and ePub files available? You can upgrade to the eBook version at `www.packt.com` and as a print book customer, you are entitled to a discount on the eBook copy. Get in touch with us at `customercare@packtpub.com` for more details.

At `www.packt.com`, you can also read a collection of free technical articles, sign up for a range of free newsletters, and receive exclusive discounts and offers on Packt books and eBooks.

Contributors

About the authors

Weimin Sun has 20 years' of experience working in the financial industry. He has worked for top-tier investment and commercial banks such as J.P. Morgan, Bank of America, Citibank, and Morgan Stanley, where he also managed large teams for developing IT applications. Weimin has also held corporate titles such as executive director and senior VP in some of these firms. Weimin has in-depth knowledge of the blockchain technology, data science, data architecture, data modeling, and big data platforms. He holds Ph.D, M.B.A and M.Sc degrees. He has co-authored *Blockchain Quick Start Guide* and published several statistical journal papers.

> *I would like to thank my wife and son for their lasting support and love.*

Xun (Brian) Wu has more than 17 years of extensive, hands-on design and development experience with blockchain, big data, cloud, UI, and systems infrastructure. He has coauthored a number of books, including *Seven NoSQL Databases in a Week*, *Blockchain by Example*, *Hyperledger Cookbook*, *Learning Ethereum*, and *Blockchain Quick Start Guide*. He has been a technical reviewer on more than 50 technical books for Packt Publishing. He serves as a board adviser for several blockchain start-ups and owns several patents on blockchain. Brian also holds an NJIT computer science M.Sc degree. He lives in New Jersey with his two beautiful daughters, Bridget and Charlotte.

> *I would like to thank my parents, wife, and kids for their patience and support throughout this endeavor.*

Angela Kwok, is a lawyer, specializing in high-tech and blockchain start-ups and venture capital financing. She also focuses on general corporate and commercial matters, fund formation, cross-border and domestic investments, mergers and acquisitions, and related tax matters in the TMT industry. She has represented clients in blockchain-related cases.

About the reviewers

Maximiliano Santos works as an architect for IBM Cloud Garage, São Paulo. He has developed complex software architectures for the banking, real estate, insurance, chemical, and consumer goods industries. Max has designed solutions using IBM Watson's cognitive services, an Internet of Things (IoT) platform, as well as machine learning and mobile applications.

Ankur Daharwal started his journey into blockchain with IBM Blockchain Garage in 2016. As a technology enthusiast and expert in both public and enterprise blockchains, he has been part of the decentralized world for around 3 years now. He has successfully developed and delivered numerous blockchain projects. He has devoted his career to devising real-life solutions for asset management and value exchange in a plethora of industry use cases worldwide. As an advisor to many blockchain startups, he focuses on providing expert guidance and solutions. Ankur strongly believes in fulfilling social responsibilities and supporting humanitarian causes with the use of his skills in technology.

Packt is searching for authors like you

If you're interested in becoming an author for Packt, please visit authors.packtpub.com and apply today. We have worked with thousands of developers and tech professionals, just like you, to help them share their insight with the global tech community. You can make a general application, apply for a specific hot topic that we are recruiting an author for, or submit your own idea.

Table of Contents

Preface 1

Chapter 1: Introduction to Blockchain 7
A brief overview of the blockchain technology 8
Bitcoin 8
Ethereum 10
Evolution of blockchain 12
Bitcoin basics 14
The distributed ledger 15
The consensus mechanism 16
Keys and digital wallets 18
Ethereum basics 19
Ethereum cryptocurrency and tokens 20
Smart contract 20
Ethereum virtual machine 22
Ethereum gas 22
Account 23
Oracle 24
Off-the-chain data 25
PoS 26
Performance considerations 26
Miscellaneous comments 27
Summary 28

Chapter 2: STO - Security Token Offering 29
A traditional fund raising roadmap for startups 30
Seed money 31
Angel investors and angel funds 31
VC fund 32
Private equity firms 33
Mezzanine capital/fund 34
IPO 35
Pros 36
Cons 36
The initial coin offering 37
Coins and tokens 38
Crowdfunding 39
ICO and its difference to IPO 41
The ICO bubble 43
The STO 47

Security   48
STO verses ICO   49
STO versus IPO   50
Challenges of STOs   52
Summary   54
Chapter 3: Monetizing Digital Tokens Under US Security Laws   55
What is an STO?   56
Overview of US securities laws   57
Federal regulations   57
Section 5 of the Securities Act of 1933   57
Section 3(b)(1) and (2) / Regulation A/A+ offerings (Mini IPOs)   58
Exemptions to Section 5 of Securities Act of 1933   59
Section 4(a)(2) / Reg D – Rule 506(b) and (c) – private placement exemption   59
Section 3(b)(1)/ Rule 504 – small issuance   60
Limitation of Rule 504 and 506 – bad actor disqualifications   61
Section 4(a)(5) – accredited investor exemption   62
Section 4(a)(6) / Regulation Crowdfunding – crowdfunding exemption   62
Section 3(a)(11) / Rule 147 (added by JOBS Act 2012) – intrastate offering   63
Regulatory issues with respect to exemptions under the Securities Act   63
Other related regulatory regimes   64
Federal regulators   66
State regulations   67
Resale of securities Rule 144/144A/Section 4(a)(1½) / Section 4(a)(7)   67
Rule 144 exemption   67
Rule 144A exemption   68
Section 4(a)(1½) exemption   68
Section 4(a)(7) exemption   68
Securities laws development in blockchain and digital
cryptocurrencies   68
SEC alerts   69
Report of Investigation Pursuant to Section 21(a) of the Exchange Act – The
DAO (July 25, 2017) (the DAO report) – the application of the Howey test   71
Legal analysis by the SEC   72
SEC's conclusion   74
Security trading   74
Real cases   74
Munchee Inc. (Munchee order, December 11, 2017)   75
Legal analysis by the SEC   75
AirFox case (November, 2018)   77
Legal analysis by the SEC   78
The Paragon case (November, 2018)   79
Legal analysis by the SEC   80
SEC versus PlexCorps et al.   82
Crypto Asset Management case (September, 2018)   83
Legal analysis by the SEC   84

The TokenLot LLC case (September, 2018)   85
Legal analysis by the SEC   86
STO launch and legal considerations   86
Summary   87
Chapter 4: Stablecoin   89
Basics of money   90
What is money?   91
Characteristics of money   93
Durability   94
Portability   94
Divisibility   95
Uniformity   95
Limited supply   96
Acceptability   96
Commodity money versus fiat currency   97
An example of a fiat currency– the USD   99
Basics of stablecoin   99
Cryptocurrency   100
What are stablecoins?   102
Are stablecoins really stable?   103
Types of stablecoins   104
Commodity-collateralized stablecoins   105
Fiat-collateralized stablecoins   106
Crypto-collateralized stablecoins   106
Non-collateralized stablecoins   107
Challenges of stablecoins   108
Summary   109
Chapter 5: Security Token Smart Contracts   111
ERC-20 and ERC-721 token   111
ERC-20   112
ERC-721 – NFTs   114
Security token technical design overview   116
ERC-1400/ERC-1410   116
ST-20 (security token standard)   119
R-Token   122
SRC-20   124
DS-Token (Securitize)   125
Securitize's digital ownership architecture   125
ERC-1404   128
ERC-884   130
Introduction to smart contracts   133
Pragma   134
Comments   135
Import   135

Paths   136
State variables   137
Functions   137
Function modifiers   138
Events   138
struct   139
enum   139
Inheritance, abstract, and interface   140
Summary   141

Chapter 6: Building a Security Token Dapp   143
STO smart contract development tools   143
Truffle   144
Ganache   144
Setting up an Ethereum development environment   146
Creating a security token Truffle project   148
Deploying security tokens to Ganache   150
Developing and testing a security token smart contract   152
Creating a smart contract   152
Implementing a smart contract   153
Defining your token information   153
Implementing detectTransferRestriction   154
Implementing messageForTransferRestriction   154
Implementing transfer and transferFrom   155
Testing a smart contract   156
Setting up and initializing the test case   156
Writing Dapp web components   162
Setting up a Dapp project   163
Cleaning boilerplates code   166
Defining the HTML template   168
Implementing the ERC1404 UI components   170
Loading accounts   170
transfer UI component   172
DetectTransferRestriction UI component   175
MessageForTransferRestriction UI component   176
AddAddressToWhitelist UI component   177
verifyWhitelist UI component   179
Summary   182

Chapter 7: Stablecoin Smart Contracts   183
Quick primary stablecoin overview   183
Timeline of stablecoin development   184
Types of stablecoin   185
Fiat collateralized stablecoins   186
Crypto collateralized stablecoins   186
Non-collateralized stablecoins   187
Stablecoin technical design overview   188

Tether (USDT)   188
TrueUSD (TUSD) smart contract   191
    modularERC20   192
    Proxy   192
    Admin   193
    Other TUSD token-related contracts 193
MakerDAO (Dai)   195
USD coin (USDC)   197
Paxos Standard   199
GUSD   203
    ERC20Proxy   204
    ERC20Impl   205
    ERC20Store   206
JPM Coin   207
Summary   209

Other Books You May Enjoy   211

Index   215

Preface

During 2017 and 2018, the market values of the majority cryptocurrencies went through some eye-popping roller-coasters. In the span of three months, the price of Bitcoin went up from $6,336.94 (USD) on November 12, 2017, to its highest price of $19,758.2 on December 17, 2017, before dropping to $7,389.79 on February 5, 2018. As cryptocurrency prices moved up, funding for blockchain projects poured in. Most of them were in the form of **initial coin offering (ICOs)**. One example is in May 2017, when a web browser called Brave completed an ICO. It raised $36 million in USD within the first 25 seconds of the ICO. The dramatic declining in cryptocurrency prices eventually led to the cooling down of the ICO madness. Per statistics from ICODATA.IO, during the first quarter of 2018, a total of $3,874 million USD were raised via ICOs. In contrast, during the first quarter of 2019, only $100 mm USD were raised through ICOs.

A fundamental reason for the high volatility in cryptocurrency prices and the ICO bubble bursting is the lack of control and regulations on ICOs. This led to a high failure rate of ICO-funded blockchain projects. Fewer than half of ICOs have survived over four months after their offerings, and nearly half (around 46%) of ICOs taking place in 2017 had failed by February 2018.

Facing the ICO issues, the blockchain community has started soul-searching for an alternative solution. The mainstream view of the blockchain community changed from focusing exclusively on the initial ICO model of raising funds, to funding models involving other parties (for example, governments, investment bankers, and lawyers). A leading solution is the **security token offering (STO)**.

To help our audience gain an overview on the context of STOs quickly, in this book, we explain the basic concepts behind the blockchain technology, traditional funding approaches for startups, and the basics of STOs. We made comparisons between ICOs and STOs to explore the differences between them and the reasons that STOs can potentially provide a viable solution to resolve some of the ICO drawbacks. To help the reader understand the implications of STOs better, we dedicate one chapter (Chapter 3, *Monetize Digital Tokens Under U.S. Securities Laws*) to covering some of applicable laws on STOs. For IT practitioners, we show a way to implement an end-to-end Dapp for the issuance of a security token. In fairness, STOs are not necessarily perfect neither. At the end of Chapter 2, *STO – Security Token Offering*, we point out some challenges faced by STOs.

Stablecoin is a solution that the blockchain community came up with to address the high volatility issue in cryptocurrency prices. In this book, we first cover the basics on money. We then proceed to illustrations on different types of money. This lays the foundation for explaining the concepts on stablecoin. In Chapter 7, *Stablecoin Smart Contracts*, we give a working example on how to implement stablecoin issuance.

Who this book is for

This book is ideal for blockchain beginners and business user developers who want to quickly master popular Security Token Offerings and stablecoins. Readers will learn how to develop blockchain/digital cryptos, guided by U.S. securities laws and utilizing some real use cases. Prior exposure to an Object-Oriented Programming language such as JavaScript would be an advantage, but is not mandatory.

What this book covers

Chapter 1, *Introduction to Blockchain*, gives an overview of blockchain technology, along with the key concepts involved, including the distributed ledger, transactions, blocks, proof of work, mining, and consensus. It covers bitcoin, the mother of blockchain technology, and Ethereum, which developed out of bitcoin, in detail.

Chapter 2, *STO – Security Token Offering*, talks about traditional fundraising methods such as angel funds, **venture capital** (**VC**) funds, private equity funds, and **initial public offerings** (**IPOs**). It then covers the blockchain project's specific funding method, ICO. Drawbacks of ICOs have been discussed as well. STO has been introduced as a promising alternative to ICO. The chapter compares STOs and ICOs. It ends by pointing out some of the challenges related to STOs.

Chapter 3, *Monetizing Digital Tokens Under U.S. Security Laws*, answers the question, "*What is an STO under U.S. securities law?*" It gives an overview of applicable U.S. securities laws, talking about the developments in U.S. securities laws related to blockchain and cryptocurrency. It then explains the process of STO launches, along with some legal considerations. The chapter mainly focus on U.S. securities laws.

Chapter 4, *Stablecoin*, talks about the definition of money, along with its basics. It then proceeds to a discussion on the concepts of cryptocurrency and stablecoins. It explains the rationale behind the implementation of stablecoins and discusses the types of stablecoins on offer. At the end, the chapter covers the challenges faced by stablecoins.

Chapter 5, *Security Token Smart Contracts*, covers popular security token standards such as ERC-1400/ERC-1410, R-Token, DS-Token, SRC-20, ST-20, S3, ERC-884, ERC-1450, and ERC-1404. The chapter helps to enrich the reader's knowledge of security token protocols. In addition, it talks about solidity programming fundamentals and explains how to write a smart contract.

Chapter 6, *Building a Security Token Dapp*, demonstrates how to develop an end-to-end product, from smart contracts to Dapp, to issuing an ERC-1404 security token. The chapter covers some basic concepts only. In a real application, the security token will be far more complex. Many security tokens run on an elaborate ecosystem and need to comply with the SEC's regulation on securities trading. For example, the security token smart contract needs to incorporate real-world legal contracts.

Chapter 7, *Stablecoin Smart Contracts*, reviews the basic features of popular stablecoins and covers three types of stablecoins, including fiat-collateralized stablecoins, crypto-collateralized stablecoins, and non-collateralized stablecoins. Then, it looks into USDT, DAI, TUSD, USDC, GUSD, and PAX stablecoin smart contract design, exploring the functions defined in these contracts. The chapter explains how each stablecoin type maintains the 1:1 price pegging through mint, burn, and other controllable functions.

To get the most out of this book

We've focused on organizing the book to fit business and IT beginners in blockchain technology. The chapters are arranged to ensure that they can be followed easily and flow naturally.

Business users can skip the chapters with detailed descriptions on how to develop STO and stablecoin applications and, instead, focus on the chapters with general descriptions of the STO and stablecoin concepts.

IT professionals should read all chapters to gain insights on the business and regulation context for STO and stablecoins, from which a reader will gain basic knowledge on how to build STO and stablecoin applications. It is recommended that IT users download the code and make modifications to adopt the code to their own use cases or exercises.

Chapter 3, *Monetize Digital Tokens Under U.S. Security Laws*, and other chapters of the book are for general knowledge of the U.S. securities laws and other laws, and shall not be considered as providing legal advice, opinions, or recommendations. For any legal issues concerning the STOs, please consult an attorney specialized in this area.

Download the example code files

You can download the example code files for this book from your account at www.packt.com. If you purchased this book elsewhere, you can visit www.packt.com/support and register to have the files emailed directly to you.

You can download the code files by following these steps:

1. Log in or register at www.packt.com.
2. Select the **SUPPORT** tab.
3. Click on **Code Downloads & Errata**.
4. Enter the name of the book in the **Search** box and follow the onscreen instructions.

Once the file is downloaded, please make sure that you unzip or extract the folder using the latest version of:

- WinRAR/7-Zip for Windows
- Zipeg/iZip/UnRarX for Mac
- 7-Zip/PeaZip for Linux

The code bundle for the book is also hosted on GitHub at https://github.com/PacktPublishing/Security-Tokens-and-Stablecoins-Quick-Start-Guide. In case there's an update to the code, it will be updated on the existing GitHub repository.

We also have other code bundles from our rich catalog of books and videos available at https://github.com/PacktPublishing/. Check them out!

Download the color images

We also provide a PDF file that has color images of the screenshots/diagrams used in this book. You can download it here: https://www.packtpub.com/sites/default/files/downloads/9781838551063_ColorImages.pdf.

Conventions used

There are a number of text conventions used throughout this book.

CodeInText: Indicates code words in text, database table names, folder names, filenames, file extensions, pathnames, dummy URLs, user input, and Twitter handles. Here is an example: "Update the truffle.js file configuration."

A block of code is set as follows:

```
module.exports = {
  networks: {
    development: {
      host: "127.0.0.1",
      port: 8545,
```

Any command-line input or output is written as follows:

```
truffle compile
```

Bold: Indicates a new term, an important word, or words that you see onscreen. For example, words in menus or dialog boxes appear in the text like this. Here is an example: "Copy the second account from the account list, and click the **Copy** button."

Warnings or important notes appear like this.

Tips and tricks appear like this.

Get in touch

Feedback from our readers is always welcome.

General feedback: If you have questions about any aspect of this book, mention the book title in the subject of your message and email us at customercare@packtpub.com.

Errata: Although we have taken every care to ensure the accuracy of our content, mistakes do happen. If you have found a mistake in this book, we would be grateful if you would report this to us. Please visit www.packt.com/submit-errata, selecting your book, clicking on the Errata Submission Form link, and entering the details.

Piracy: If you come across any illegal copies of our works in any form on the Internet, we would be grateful if you would provide us with the location address or website name. Please contact us at copyright@packt.com with a link to the material.

If you are interested in becoming an author: If there is a topic that you have expertise in and you are interested in either writing or contributing to a book, please visit `authors.packtpub.com`.

Reviews

Please leave a review. Once you have read and used this book, why not leave a review on the site that you purchased it from? Potential readers can then see and use your unbiased opinion to make purchase decisions, we at Packt can understand what you think about our products, and our authors can see your feedback on their book. Thank you!

For more information about Packt, please visit `packt.com`.

1
Introduction to Blockchain

In this chapter, we give an overview of blockchain technology, along with its key concepts, such as the distributed ledger, transactions, blocks, proof of work, mining, consensus, and so on. We will cover bitcoin, the mother of blockchain technology, and Ethereum, which was developed out of bitcoin, in detail. We will then proceed to the discussion of **initial coin offerings (ICOs)** and **security token offerings (STOs)** in Chapter 2, *STO – Security Token Offering*. Chapter 3, *Monetizing Digital Tokens Under US Security Laws*, is dedicated to STO-related laws and regulations. We will cover the basics on stablecoins in Chapter 4, *Stablecoin*. Chapter 5, *Security Token Smart Contracts*, and Chapter 6, *Building a Security Token Dapp*, demonstrate how to build frontend and backend applications to issue security tokens, along with examples. The last two chapters talk about how to build a stablecoins frontend and backend applications.

In this chapter, we cover the following specific topics:

- A brief overview of the blockchain technology
- Bitcoin basics
- Ethereum basics
- Miscellaneous comments

A brief overview of the blockchain technology

In October 2008, Satoshi Nakamoto published a landmark white paper titled *Bitcoin: A Peer-to-Peer Electronic Cash System*. Although the true identity of Satoshi has not been ;revealed, this paper triggered a gold rush to cryptocurrency and led to the birth of a new technology—blockchain. While the initial rush to cryptocurrency has suffered a severe setback due to dramatically descending prices of main cryptocurrencies such as BTC (bitcoin), XRP (Ripple), and ether (Ethereum), blockchain as a technology is alive. Numerous blockchain projects are being worked on worldwide. The technology will fundamentally change the way most businesses will be conducted and how people will live. ICOs, a primary fundraising method used in the cryptocurrency and blockchain world, have played the main role in this gold rush, driving up the BTC's price to an unprecedented level, by over USD 19,000 in December, 2017. The cryptocurrency bubble burst in late 2018 as BTC's price crashed. It is below $4,000 as of January, 2019. The dramatic drop in price of the main cryptocurrencies led to the death of ICOs.

It is not coincidental that the ICO bubble burst. A similar event occurred in the financial world over ten years ago—the 2008 financial crisis. The primary reason for the 2008 crisis was the lack of control in lending standards, resulting in the issuances of many loans to unqualified borrowers. The loans were then packaged via a financial-engineering process called **securitization**, and sold to unsuspecting investors worldwide. When enough borrowers started to default on their mortgages, a worldwide financial crisis broke out. The ICO fundraising model is fundamentally flawed in its lack of control on many of the proposed projects, for which funds were raised. Via an ICO, an entrepreneur can raise tens of millions of US dollars within minutes without a real product or even a company! All it has is a white paper, sometimes only a few pages long. To address the issues of ICOs and support the blockchain industry's future growth, the blockchain community has proposed and promoted the STO idea. STO has attracted a lot of attention and it is expected to play a promising role in the replacement of ICOs.

Bitcoin

In his paper, Satoshi Nakamoto pioneered a way to integrate several key ingredients and develop an electronic payment application. This application offers a more efficient and low-cost solution to fulfill a payment through the removal of intermediaries. These key ingredients include digital money, encryption, decentralization, consensus mechanism, chained blocks, and a peer-to-peer network. Many people responded to Satoshi's idea. They formed the core team to implement the idea.

In January 2009, Satoshi Nakamoto released the first software and blockchain platform. This blockchain platform is referred to as **bitcoin**, which minted the first coins of the bitcoin cryptocurrency—BTC coins. Many of the key ingredients have evolved. Satoshi's main contribution is to put them together to address the pain points of the existing business model, such as high cost and long execution time for facilitating cross-border payments.

When relying on an existing business solution, it usually takes three days to complete a cross-border payment transaction. With Satoshi's proposed solution or its variations, it takes a few minutes or seconds to finish the same transaction at a tiny fraction of the costs of non-blockchain-based solutions.

For the rest of our discussions, we will use the term **blockchain industry** to refer to both cryptocurrency and blockchain technology. The word *blockchain* refers to a sequence of encrypted blocks chained linearly. Bitcoin's platform shares many of the same characteristics as a genealogy tree. They are summarized as follows:

- Like a clan consisting of many related families, a blockchain network (a clan) consists of nodes. Each node is like a family.
- While every family keeps a copy of the clan's genealogy, each bitcoin node maintains a copy of all transactions that occurred on the chain, starting from the very beginning. The collection of all these transactions is a **distributed ledger**. Since every node keeps a copy of the ledger, blockchain is essentially a decentralized data repository.
- A genealogy starts with a common ancestor of the clan. The ancestor has offspring. The equivalent of a common ancestor is called the **genesis block**. The genesis block is followed by one child block, which, in turn, is followed by its own child block, and so on. The collection of all blocks is the blockchain (or in business terms, the ledger). Each block contains one or multiple transactions.
- Adding a new name to a genealogy requires a consensus of families within a clan. Similarly, bitcoin relies on a consensus mechanism to decide whether a newly built block is valid, and can be added to the chain.
- Like a genealogy, after a block is added to a chain, it is difficult to change. This is the **immutability** feature of bitcoin.
- Genealogy provides transparency regarding a clan's history. Similarly, a blockchain allows a user to query the ledger on BTC transactions. This is bitcoin's **transparency** feature.

The bitcoin blockchain design is restricted to resolve one specific business problem—the cash payment. Its value is therefore limited. A generic blockchain platform, called **Ethereum**, is then implemented by adding new ingredients such as smart contracts, as well as generic programming languages.

Ethereum

As is being pointed out, bitcoin has shortcomings, such as the following:

- Bitcoin serves a specific purpose—cash payment.
- Bitcoin's scripting language is not Turing complete; for example, it has no looping statement, and so on. Here, the Turing completeness refers to the ability of a programming language to resolve any computational problems.
- Bitcoin does not have a state. Consequently, to answer a question such as *What is the total number of minted BTCs?*, you have to search the entire ledger.

To address these issues, Vitalik Buterin, a Canadian cryptocurrency researcher and programmer, proposed the idea of Ethereum in late 2013. Funded by an online crowdfunding sale—an ICO—the system went live on July 30, 2015, with 11.9 million coins **premined** for the crowdsale.

The core idea for Ethereum is to implement a general purpose blockchain. With that, users can address a wide range of business problems. Ethereum introduced a few key concepts:

- A **Turing complete** programming language, such as **Solidity**.
- Smart contracts, which define business logic and are deployed on the blockchain—every node maintains and runs the same code at almost the same time. Thus, smart contracts are immutable and are guaranteed to be executed and yield the same outcomes.

The idea of Solidity was initially proposed in August 2014 by Gavin Wood. The Ethereum project's Solidity team led by Christian Reitwiessner later developed the language. It is one of the four languages (Solidity, Serpent, **Lisp Like Language** (**LLL**), Viper, and Mutan) that was designed for **Ethereum virtual machine** (**EVM**).

The introduction of the smart contract concept, along with others, has significant implications:

- A smart contract is a scripted legal document, since it is immutable and enforceable.
- The code built into the contract is stored on the Ethereum blockchain and cannot be tampered with or removed. This makes the scripted legal document credible.
- After being triggered, smart contracts cannot be stopped, meaning no one can easily influence the running code. As long as triggering conditions are met, the code will be guaranteed to run and the legally defined actions will be fulfilled.

- Ethereum to blockchain is like an OS to a computer. In other words, the Ethereum is a general purpose platform.
- It now has a Turing complete language—Solidity.

Bitcoin and Ethereum, along with many of their variations, are collectively called **public blockchain**, since they are open to everyone who is interested in participating in the network. No approval is required. Public blockchains cannot satisfy the needs of many companies. As per these firms' business models, a participant has to receive approval before being authorized to join a network. To satisfy their needs, **private blockchain** platforms are implemented by modifying public blockchain platforms such as Ethereum and adding an authorization and entitlement component.

Since the membership of a private blockchain network is tightly controlled, several things can be simplified. For example, the consensus algorithm is simplified. Consequently, a primary blockchain platform has much better performance. Also, a private blockchain does not require that you issue a coin so that it gets its work done. Hyperledger is a well-known private blockchain. It is also referred to as an **enterprise blockchain**.

Ethereum greatly expanded the blockchain technology's capabilities. However, there are many scenarios where Ethereum is not enough, as we just pointed out. The issues of Ethereum are restated here:

- Enterprise applications, for example, credit card transactions, require high-performance, as there are potentially billions of transactions a day. The current form of Ethereum has a maximum capacity of handling around 1.4 million transactions a day. Bitcoin is even worse: 300,000 transactions a day.
- Many financial markets, for instance, **over-the-counter** (**OTC**) derivatives or foreign exchange contracts, are permission-based. A public blockchain supported by Ethereum or bitcoin does not satisfy such a need.

Big companies across industries are addressing these issues. They form consortia to work on enterprise blockchain projects. With a permission-based enterprise blockchain network, a node has to receive approval before it can join the network. Hyperledger is one of them.

The **Linux Foundation** (**LF**) created the Hyperledger project in December 2015. Its objective is to advance cross-industry collaboration by developing blockchains and distributed ledgers. On July 12, 2017, the project announced its production-ready **Hyperledger Fabric** (**HF**) 1.0.

Currently, Hyperledger includes five blockchain frameworks:

- **HF**: A private blockchain, initially contributed by IBM and Digital Asset, is designed to be a foundation for developing applications or solutions with a modular architecture. It takes plugin components to provide functionalities such as consensus and membership services. Like Ethereum, HF can host and execute smart contracts. However, HF uses the term **chaincode** instead of smart contract. An HF network consists of peer nodes, which execute smart contracts (chaincode), query ledger data, validate transactions, and interact with applications. Transactions entered by users are channeled to an ordering-service component, which essentially serves to be HF's consensus mechanism. Special nodes called **orderer nodes** validate the transactions and ensure the consistency of the blockchain and send the validated transactions to peer nodes, as well as to **Membership Service Provider** (**MSP**) services. MSP is the certificate authority.
- **Hyperledger Iroha**: Based on HF, it is designed for mobile applications. Iroha was contributed by Soramitsu, Hitachi, NTT Data, and Colu. It implemented a consensus algorithm called **Sumeragi**.
- **Hyperledger Burrow**: Contributed initially by Monax and Intel, Burrow is a modular blockchain that was client-built to follow EVM specifications.
- **Hyperledger Sawtooth**: Contributed to by Intel, it implemented a consensus algorithm called **Proof of Elapsed Time** (**PoET**). PoET was invented by Intel and is designed to achieve distributed consensus as efficiently as possible. **Sawtooth** supports both permissioned and permissionless networks. Sawtooth is designed for versatility.
- **Hyperledger Indy**: Initially contributed by the Sovrin Foundation, it is to support independent identity on distributed ledgers. Indy provides tools, libraries, and reusable components to support digital identities.

Evolution of blockchain

The blockchain technology is still in its early stages. It may take many years before it becomes mature and its potential has been fully explored. At the moment, there is no universally agreed way to classify generations for the technology.

In her book on blockchain, Melanie Swan defined blockchain 1.0 – 3.0. According to her view, these phases can be described as follows:

- Blockchain 1.0 refers to the cryptocurrency phase. During this phase, the blockchain applications focus mainly on cash payment, such as currency transfer, remittance, and digital payment systems.
- Blockchain 2.0 refers to the smart contract phase. During this phase, the blockchain applications focus in certain areas of the financial industry, for example, currency, financing, and security markets.
- Blockchain 3.0 refers to the blockchain technology being applied to areas beyond currency, financing, and security markets. For example, blockchain technology is utilized in areas such as non-profit organization causes, the health industry, the supply chain, manufacturing activities, and so on.

Some others divided the blockchain evolution into four generations:

- **Blockchain 1.0**: Bitcoin is the most prominent example. Financial transactions are executed based on **distributed ledger technology (DLT)**. Cryptocurrency is used as cash for the internet.
- **Blockchain 2.0**: Ethereum is the most prominent example. The key concept is smart contracts, which are stored and executed on a blockchain.
- **Blockchain 3.0**: The keyword is **Dapps (decentralized applications)**. Dapps use decentralized storage and decentralized communication. Unlike a smart contract, which only involves a backend or server-side code, a Dapp can have a frontend code, also called **client-side code**, for example, user interfaces, to interact with its backend code in a blockchain. In summary, Dapp is a frontend and has smart contracts.
- **Blockchain 4.0**: Blockchain platforms are being built to serve **Industry 4.0**. Industry 4.0 refers to automation, enterprise resource planning, and the integration of different execution systems.

Regardless of how the generations are defined, it is certain that the growth of this technology is far from over. New ideas and implementations will be incorporated into the existing platforms to deal with challenges from real-life problems. In other words, blockchain technology will be nimble and is self-adjusted to be an enabler in resolving business problems.

Issuing a cryptocurrency or a token is more relevant to public blockchains. In the next two sections, we discuss bitcoin and Ethereum in detail.

Bitcoin basics

The bitcoin platform is a peer-to-peer network. It connects computers around the world. Each computer is a **node** with equal status, except for a subset of nodes called **miners**. Mining nodes play the role of collecting/validating transactions, creating a new block, and adding a validated block to the blockchain. A transaction refers to an action such as issuing bitcoin or transferring BTC from one address to another, and so on.

A peer-to-peer network can connect worldwide nodes and allow participants to trade with one another. However, the physical connection is not enough to make two untrusting parties trade with each other. To make them trade, bitcoin takes the following measures:

- Every node saves a complete copy of the ledger. Thus, any alteration to a transaction on the chain becomes practically not feasible.
- Transactions are grouped into blocks. A non-genesis block is linked to its previous block by storing that block's hash. Consequently, a change to a transaction requires changes to be made to all subsequent blocks, and these changes have to be repeated on all nodes where a copy of the ledger is saved. This clever design makes hacking the distributed ledger extremely difficult.
- Bitcoin built in a consensus mechanism to address the double-spending issue; that is, the same BTC is spent twice.
- Hashes are extensively used to protect identities of parties, and to detect any changes that are occurring in a block.
- It uses public/private keys and addresses to mask identities of trading parties.
- Signs a transaction digitally.

With these measures, untrusting parties feel comfortable to trade because of the following reasons:

- The transaction is immutable and permanent. Neither party can nullify a transaction unilaterally.
- No double-spending is possible.
- Transaction and settlement occur simultaneously; therefore, there is no settlement risk.
- Identities are protected.
- Transactions are signed by both parties, which minimizes the possibility of legal disputes in the future.

The distributed ledger

At a financial institution, the ledger is the principal book for recording all financial transactions. Bitcoin maintains a ledger for bookkeeping transactions of coins and other transactions. The difference is that a bank's ledger is centralized, and bitcoin's ledger is distributed. Consequently, a bank's ledger is at risk of being manipulated for nefarious purposes, that is, *cooking the book.* On the other hand, bitcoin's ledger is very difficult to be changed.

Blockchain's ledger consists of entries resulting from transactions entered by users, where users submit transactions. Each transaction contains the following information:

- Sources (from the address) of the coins to be transferred from
- The number of coins to be transferred
- Destinations (send-to address) where coins should be transferred to

Both source and destination addresses are 64-character hashes. Here is an example:

```
979e6b063b436438105895939f4ff13d068428d2f71312cf5594c132905bfxy1
```

An address is like a customer's bank account number. However, there are fundamental differences between them. For example, a bank has a centralized place for saving metadata on an account, for example, the customer name, account open date, and account type, and so on. Also, the balance of an account is calculated and saved. A bitcoin address does not have metadata and maintains no balance. Addresses are referred to only in bitcoin transactions. When an address does not contain any unused coins, a new request for transferring a coin from the address will fail a transaction validation due to an *insufficient fund* error.

A bitcoin coin does not associate with a physical object such as a file or a physical coin. Only transactions and addresses support its existence. For example, if you want to know the total number of coins that have been minted so far, you have to go through all addresses with unused coins and add them up.

When a user enters a transaction request at a node, bitcoin software installed at the node broadcasts the transaction to all nodes. Nodes on the network will validate the transaction by retrieving all historical transactions containing the input addresses and ensuring that coins that are transferred out from these addresses are legitimate and sufficient. After that, the mining nodes start to construct a block by collecting the validated transactions. Normally, one block contains between 1,500 and 2,000 transactions. If a miner wins a race for resolving a difficult puzzle, the miner gets the role for adding the new block to the blockchain. Bitcoin takes approximately every 10 minutes to add a new block.

A bitcoin blockchain can diverge due to protocol change, software upgrade, or fixing hacked blocks. The splitting point where the divergence starts is called a **fork**. There are temporary forks and permanent forks. If a permanent fork occurs due to, for example, malicious attacks, it is called a **hard fork**. If a permanent fork occurs due to configuration or a software upgrade, it is called a **soft fork**. A hard fork makes previously invalid blocks/transactions valid, and a soft fork makes previously valid blocks/transactions invalid.

The consensus mechanism

The double-spending issue refers to the act of using the same coin more than once. If this problem is not resolved, a bitcoin coin loses its scarcity. Scarcity is a key feature of a currency. Without it, the coin can no longer be called a cryptocurrency. The consensus mechanism is designed for resolving the double-spending problem. To understand how the mechanism works, you need to know the concepts of **proof of work** (**PoW**) and mining.

As we learned earlier, a miner has to solve a mathematical puzzle ahead of other miners to receive the role of being a builder of the next block and receive an award for doing the work. The work of resolving the mathematical problem is called the PoW. The mathematical problem itself does not have a value. The main purpose is to give a sufficient window of time to miners validating transactions. This window of waiting time is maintained at 10 minutes. A miner can query its copy of the distributed ledger and validate the following facts:

- The requester of a transaction has the coins
- Any other transactions in the ledger have not spent the same coins
- Other transactions within the candidate block do not spend the same coins

The process of repeatedly guessing an answer to the puzzle is called **mining**. Hardware that is manufactured and dedicated to the mining work is called a **mining rig**.

As per bitcoin protocol, mining is the only way to issue a new coin. Rewarding a miner serves several purposes:

- Compensates a miner's investments on hardware
- Covers mining operation costs such as utility bills, human salaries, site rentals, and so on
- Gives miners incentives to safeguard the network from being attacked by malicious hackers

The total number of mintable bitcoin coins is fixed at 21 million. Currently (January 2019), close to 17.5 million coins have been issued. The bitcoin protocol defines a rule for dynamically adjusting the payout rate to the mining work, and the remaining 3.5 million coins will need another 122 years to be mined completely.

The mining payout rate is dynamically adjusted and follows the following rule:

The rate changes at every 210,000 blocks. It is a function of the block height on the chain with genesis=0, and is calculated using 64-bit integer operations as *(50 * 100,000,000) >> (height / 210,000)*. The rate that initially started with 50 coins has fallen to 25 coins at block 210,000. It fell to 12.5 coins at block 420,000 and will eventually go down to 0 when the network reaches the size of 6,930,000 blocks.

Bitcoin adjusts the **difficulty level** of the puzzle for maintaining the 10-minute window. Based on the most recent rate of a new block being added, the difficulty level is calculated or adjusted accordingly. If the average rate of new blocks being added is fewer than ten minutes, the difficulty level will be increased. If the average rate takes more than ten minutes, it's decreased. The difficulty level is updated every 2,016 blocks.

With the relevant concepts being explained, we are ready to talk about the mining steps. For illustration purposes, we assume that the mathematical puzzle is to find the first hash value whose first character is 0 in order to maintain the 10-minute per new block window. Per the bitcoin protocol, a miner follows these steps to solve the puzzle:

1. First, obtain the SHA-256 hash of a block in construction.
2. If the resulted hash has a leading 0, the miner solves the puzzle. The miner adds the block to his/her copy of the distributed ledger on the node and claims the coin rewards. The winner broadcasts the news to other nodes. Other miners of the network check the answer and validate that the new block contains valid transactions.
3. If passing the checks, all nodes on the network add the block to their copies of the ledger. Miners start to work on the next block.
4. If the winner is a hacker and includes bad transactions such as double-spending a coin, the validation on transactions will fail. Other miners will not include the block in their ledger copies. They will continue to mine on the current block. As time passes, the path containing the bad block will no longer be the longest path. Per bitcoin protocol, the longest path is considered to be the blockchain and should be copied by all nodes. In other words, the path containing the bad block becomes an orphan, and will eventually be dropped. This is essentially how all nodes on the network reach a consensus to add only good blocks to the blockchain and prevent bad blocks from being included.

5. If the resulted hash does not start with 0, per protocol, a miner adds a sequence number, known to be a nonce, starting from 0 at the end of the input text and retries the hash.

6. If a resulted hash still does not contain a leading 0, change the nonce to 1, and obtain a new hash. Repeat the steps until a miner finds a new hash with a leading zero.

The following is a hypothetical example. The original plaintext is `input string` and a nonce varying from 0 to 3. Their corresponding SHA-256 hashes are as follows:

- `input string`:
  `f23f4781d6814ebe349c6b230c1f700714f4f70f735022bd4b1fb69421859993`

- `input string0`:
  `5db70bb3ae36e5b87415c1c9399100bc60f2068a2b0ec04536e92ad2598b6bbb`

- `input string1`:
  `5d0a0f2c69b88343ba44d64168b350ef62ce4e0da73044557bff451fd5df6e96`

- `input string2`:
  `7b8fe11e193f835e37301f20416c76c9cd55d962a5ad009f4302ee2607ba8d1a`

- `input string3`:
  `c37e5a2e94575060277e3b1abf9d3ebbe44274e72bb86f2a526266c9c5aa3722`

The algorithm for adjusting the difficulty level is to change the required number of leading 0s, along with some minor tuning. Requiring additional leading 0s will increase the average trying times, and therefore the difficulty level is higher. The current bitcoin difficulty level is 18 leading 0s to maintain the 10 minute window.

Keys and digital wallets

When a bitcoin address is created, a pair of public and private keys are generated as well. The public key is made known to the public, and the address owner keeps the private key. To spend coins associated with the address, the owner provides a digital signature that's generated with the private key and sends a transaction request to the network. In other words, you have to pose both the address and the private key to spend the corresponding coins.

If an owner loses the address and the private key, the person then permanently loses the coins. Hence, it is important to save the information at a secured place. Digital wallets are available for assisting users in managing public/private keys and addresses. You can use a wallet to do the following:

- Generate addresses and their corresponding public/private keys
- Save and organize information such as keys, addresses, coins owned, and so on
- Send a transaction request to the bitcoin network

A private key is a 256-bit long hash, and a public key is 512-bit long.

They can be converted into shorter lengths in hexadecimal representation. The following screenshot is a pair of sample public/private keys, along with an address:

```
Private key:
a7f9c7ad318014b11cbad0a18587b374c339d91f55ca64c4c5e067776d0b65cb

Public key:
04d8fc7523fcd7caa825b6ed97d8564c78f59e8ba903bff5fe1e3c096a45d435937
942616f4dbccb353d3e19e822d707996143a603a6273cf237acfaf5bd029874

Wif:    5K6GJ5y9qSDSmrGZ1idLbWoXk4iaJpxFuDpiCC78cgngCXTSeDv

Address:   1GnUipq7cTjiPxEsCDzW6nYgbUyRa7eFYm
```

A private key can also be expressed in a string of 51 characters starting with a 5 and a public key in a string of 72 characters. Here are some examples:

```
private key:
5Jd54v5mVLvyRsjDGTFbTZFGvwLosYKayRosbLYMxZFBLfEpXnp;
public key:
BFCDB2DCE28D959F2815B16F81798483ADA7726A3C4655DA4FBFC0E1108A8FD17B448A68
```

Ethereum basics

Ethereum was developed on top of the bitcoin blockchain and shares many key features, such as the distributed ledger and PoW, and so on. However, Ethereum introduces new and critical ingredients. In this section, we will cover them, along with other useful facts.

Ethereum cryptocurrency and tokens

Ether is Ethereum's native cryptocurrency. In other words, ether to Ethereum is like BTC to bitcoin. Due to the forking for handling a hacking event in 2016, two competing Ethereum coins were generated, and both are currently traded at cryptocurrency markets. Their symbols are Ethereum (ETH) and Ethereum Classic (ETC). ETH is priced a lot higher than ETC.

Unlike BTC (that has only one denomination but can be divided into fractions), ether has many denominations. An ether is the biggest unit. The smallest unit is a Wei, named after a digital money pioneer, Wei Dai. Wei invented **B-money**. Other units include a Gwei, microether, and milliether. They are known by other names as well. For example, a milliether is also called Finney, named after another digital money pioneer, Harold Thomas Finney II, who in 2004 implemented the world's first cryptocurrency, **reusable proofs of work (RPOW)** before bitcoin. The following table lists conversion rates between ether and other units:

Denominations		
Unit	**Wei Value**	**Wei**
Gwei (shannon)	1e9 wei	1,000,000,000
microether (szabo)	1e12 wei	1,000,000,000,000
milliether (finney)	1e15 wei	1,000,000,000,000,000
ether	1e18 wei	1,000,000,000,000,000,000

In addition to the native cryptocurrency, Ethereum allows users to issue their tokens. The issuance of a customized token needs to follow predefined technical standards. One well-known standard is the **ERC-20** token. **ERC** refers to **Ethereum Request for Comment**, and 20 is the number assigned to the request. ERC-20 standard defines a list of rules for issuing ERC-20 tokens. By doing so, it allows for interaction and conversion among Ethereum tokens, and also with Ether. There are many other standards, for example, ERC-223, ERC-721, and so on.

Smart contract

In 1994, Nick Szabo first used the term **smart contract**. Szabo is a computer scientist and the inventor of Bit Gold. In his blog, Nick Szabo describes it as similar to the vending machine, which is the granddaddy of all smart contracts. A vending machine is built with hard-coded rules that define what actions are to be executed when certain conditions are fulfilled. For example:

- If Susan inserts a dollar bill, then she will receive a bag of pretzels
- If Tom inserts a five-dollar bill, then Tom will receive a bag of pretzels and change of four dollars

In other words, rules are defined and enforced by a vending machine physically. Similarly, a smart contract contains rules in program code that are triggered and run on the Ethereum platform when certain conditions are met.

Some important facts about smart contracts are summarized as follows:

- A smart contract is immutable.
- A smart contract is permanent.
- A smart contract is timestamped.
- A smart contract is globally available.
- A smart contract is a digitized legal document.
- A smart contract defines the protocol for facilitating, verifying, or enforcing an agreement among trading parties.
- Smart contracts allow for the execution of transactions without an intermediary. The transactions are auditable and irreversible.
- Smart contracts are applicable in many cases.
- For deploying and running a smart contract, you need to sign it digitally.
- Smart contract code is visible to everyone. This makes smart contracts vulnerable, as a hacker can tap the flaws in the code and initiate vicious attacks.

Ethereum virtual machine

An Ethereum's smart contract can be developed in one of four languages: **Solidity** (inspired by JavaScript), **Serpent** (inspired by Python, and no longer used), LLL (inspired by Lisp), and **Mutan** (inspired by Go, and no longer used). Since all of them are high-level programming languages, smart contracts need to be compiled into a low-level, machine-runnable language. Ethereum uses a VM approach, similar to the concept of **Java Virtual Machine** (**JVM**), to meet this need. The Ethereum erosion of VM is called **EVM**. Smart contract codes are converted to EVM-runnable bytecodes called **opcode**. The opcode is then deployed to the Ethereum blockchain for execution. Furthermore, currently, a research-oriented language is under development, called Viper—a strongly-typed Python-based language.

Ethereum gas

An Ethereum transaction can call a smart contract, which can, in turn, call another smart contract and then another, and so on. Thus, an improperly written smart contract may lead to circular calls and result in infinite loops. Stopping a smart contract infinite loop is almost impossible, since thousands of nodes worldwide run the same looping code. To stop the infinite loop, all running nodes need to be shut down within a short time window. Even if one node fails to comply, the infinite loop is still alive. When other nodes are back to the network, the running infinite loop is brought back to these nodes as well. It is a logistical nightmare to coordinate and shut down all nodes worldwide at approximately the same time.

To resolve this issue, the concept of **gas** was introduced. A vehicle relies on an engine, which depends on gas for energy. If an engine runs out of gas, the vehicle stops. When a transaction is submitted, a requester is required to provide the max gas amount. Each execution step of a smart contract uses a certain amount of gas. An infinite-looping smart contract will eventually lead to the maximum gas amount being used up, and a node will no longer execute the contract. Another advantage of using gas is that it makes hacking prohibitively expensive and, therefore, deters hacking activities.

Gas is a metering unit for measuring consumption just like a kilowatt is the unit for measuring electricity usage. Suppose in a month a family uses 210 KW. Before sending a bill to the family, the utility company first converts 210 KW into US dollars based on a predefined conversion rate. Suppose a unit of KW costs $0.20 USD; the total charge for the month is $0.2 \times 210 = \$42$ USD.

Similarly, gas usage is converted into ether for being charged to a requestor. Ethereum allows a requester to specify the conversion rate when the transaction is submitted. A validator (Ethereum's equivalent to the miner for bitcoin) has the option of giving a preference to transactions with higher rates. If a requester does not specify a rate, EVM uses a default rate, which varies. For example, in 2016, the rate for 1 gas was 0.00001 ETH. In 2018, 1 gas was 0.00000002 ETH.

Account

Unlike bitcoin where the term **address** is used, Ethereum uses the term **account**. However, Ethereum accounts can have addresses. That is, for bitcoin, the concepts of account and address are combined into one, while Ethereum separates them. Ethereum supports two types of accounts: externally owned accounts (owned by users who keep private keys of the accounts) and contract accounts.

The key facts about externally controlled accounts are listed as follows:

- They maintain ether balances
- They can initiate transactions for either transferring ether coins or triggering smart contracts
- They are controlled by users via private keys
- They have no associated smart contract code

Facts about contract accounts are as follows:

- They keep ether balances
- They have associated smart contract code
- Smart contract code execution is triggered by transactions or calls that are received from other contracts

For both types of accounts, they consist of four components:

- **Nonce**: For an externally owned account, it refers to the number of transactions sent from the account; for a contract account, it is the number of contracts associated with the account
- **Balance**: It is the number of Wei owned by this account
- **StorageRoot**: A 256-bit hash of contents of an account
- **CodeHash**: The hash of the code of this account in EVM—this is the code that gets executed when the code is called

When ether is transferred from contract accounts to an externally owned account, there is a fee, for example, 21,000 unit of gas. When ether is sent from an externally owned account to a contract account, the fee is usually higher, which depends on the smart contract code and the data being sent along with the transaction.

Ethereum addresses of accounts have the following format:

- They start with the prefix 0x, a common identifier for hexadecimal, followed by the number string to be constructed by following these steps:
    1. First, take the Keccak-256 hash (big-endian) of the **elliptic curve digital signature algorithm (ECDSA)** public key
    2. Then, take the last 20 bytes of the hash

Since, in hexadecimal, two digits are stored in one byte, a 20-bytes address is represented with 40 hexadecimal digits. The following is an example of an Ethereum address: 0xe99356bde974bbe08721d77712168fa074279267.

With a browsing tool, you can retrieve Ethereum account balances. For example, you can go to https://www.etherchain.org to obtain the top account balances in ether.

Oracle

Ethereum smart contracts are executed on nodes worldwide. To yield the same outcomes, nodes have to take the same set of inputs. This is called **determinism**. Ethereum relies on the determinism property validating smart contract outputs. That is, validating nodes have to yield the same results while running the same code. In this sense, the determinism property plays a key role in enabling nodes reaching a consensus.

Maintaining determinism can be a challenging task. On the one side, Ethereum is a general-purpose platform. Its smart contracts require data or inputs from external sources such as the internet. Without access to these sources of information, use cases for smart contracts will be restrictive. On the other side, even with a tiny time difference, validating nodes may retrieve different information from an external source. With different inputs, nodes will end up with different outputs.

Consequently, the determinism property does not hold. For avoiding the issue, smart contracts are not permitted to call an internet URL or pull data from an external source directly. To resolve the paradox, Ethereum relies on **Oracle**.

A definition of Oracle is as follows:

> *"A shrine in which a deity reveals hidden knowledge or the divine purpose through such a person."*
>
> *– Merriam-Webster*

In blockchain, *oracle* refers to the third-party or decentralized data feed services that provide external data. Oracle provides interfaces from the real world to the digital world. Oracle data is not part of blockchain and is available off-chain.

There are different types of oracles. Two of them are software oracles and hardware oracles:

- **Software oracles**: This normally refers to easily accessible online information such as stock index prices, FX rates, economic news, weather forecasts, and so on. Software oracles are useful since they provide smart contracts with a wide range of information and up-to-date data.
- **Hardware oracles**: This normally refers to scanned information such as UPS delivery scanning, registered mail scanning, supplier goods delivery scanning, and so on. This feed can be useful to activate a smart contract acting on an event's occurrence.

Off-the-chain data

There are multiple scenarios where data cannot be stored on a chain:

- **State variables**: Data stored on an Ethereum blockchain is immutable. However, contents of state variables vary as account balances change. A solution is to save them off-the-chain.
- **Oracle**: We have just talked about that.
- **Digitized assets**: Commonly digitized assets require a large dataset to describe/define them. Given a limited size of blocks, it is not feasible for hosting complete asset information on a chain.
- **Trimmed blocks**: For optimization, Ethereum full nodes need to keep a portion of the distributed ledger, that is, to trim a ledger. The trimmed blocks are saved off-the-chain at a centralized location for supporting future inquiries.

PoS

Proof of Stake (PoS) is an algorithm for choosing a validator to build the next block. Per the PoS algorithm, when a validator owns more coins, the validator has a higher chance to be chosen. Compared to PoW, PoS is much more energy efficient and quicker.

A pure PoS will lead to the richest validator being selected frequently, causing a **supernode** problem, referring to a node validating the majority of the blocks being added to the chain. This obviously will not work. Additional randomness is required to give other validators better chances. Several randomization methods are available:

- **Randomized block selection**: Uses a formula to look for the lowest hash value in combination with the size of the stake for selecting a validator.
- **Coin age-based selection**: Coins owned long enough, say 30 days, are eligible to compete for the next block. A validator with older and larger sets of coins have a better chance of being granted the role.
- **Delegated PoS**: This implementation chooses a limited number of nodes to propose and validate blocks being added to the blockchain.
- **Randomized PoS**: Each node is selected randomly using a verifiable random beacon for building the new block.

Ethereum is working on replacing PoW with PoS in future releases.

Performance considerations

Ethereum is inherently slow. The average waiting time for a validator building a block is 17 seconds. It usually requires 12 blocks in depth before a transaction (containing the first block) is confirmed. This is $12 \times 17 = 204$ seconds or 3.4 minutes of waiting time for a transaction to be confirmed. The **12-blocks-in-depth rule** is necessary. When a block is newly added to the blockchain by a validator to its ledger copy, there could be a competing path worked on by other validators. The validator may lose the competition for building the longest blockchain. Per blockchain protocol, the validator has to drop its own block being worked on and add the winning block to its ledger copy. The 12-blocks-in-depth rule assures that a transaction does not end up in a block to be dropped later.

Throughput is a measure of how many units of information a system can process in a given time window. For measuring the performance of a transaction platform, the throughput is expressed in terms of **throughput per second** (**TPS**). To calculate Ethereum TPS, we take the approximate number of transactions in a block (using 2,000). Then, we divide it by the waiting time in seconds for a transaction to be confirmed, 204 seconds. So, Ethereum TPS is approximately 9.8, that is, almost 10 transactions per second. By applying the same approach, we can estimate the TPS for bitcoin, which is about 0.5 transaction per second. On the other hand, Visa has a TPS of 2,000 with a peak TPS of 40,000. A high performance database such as VoltDB can handle over a million insertions a second. A stock exchange can match thousands of trades a second. It clearly shows a gap that needs to be closed by the blockchain community.

Ethereum is working on multiple solutions to increase TPS. PoS is worked on as a replacement of the computationally inefficient PoW algorithm. PoS is not fully implemented and upgraded on mainnet due to concerns regarding the emergence of a set of supernodes (which receive an outsized role in building the new blocks). **Casper** is the Ethereum community's attempt to transiting out of PoW and into PoS. Per Casper protocol, validators set aside a portion of their ether as a stake. When a validator identifies a candidate block, ether is bet on that block by the validator. If the block is indeed added to the chain, the validator is rewarded based on the size of its bet. Validators acting maliciously will be penalized by having their stakes removed.

Led by Vitalik, the Ethereum Foundation is also working on the **sharding** approach, which is aiming at increasing TPS by 80 times. Sharding splits up the state of the network into multiple shards, where each shard has its transaction history and portion of the network's state.

Another idea to increase TPS is **Plasma**. Plasma is a technique for conducting off-the-chain transactions while relying on the underlying Ethereum blockchain to provide its security. Therefore, Plasma belongs to the group of off-chain technologies. **Truebit** is another example of this.

Miscellaneous comments

Ethereum has three main ingredients:

- **Decentralization**: For guaranteed execution
- **Hashes**: For safeguarding the world state
- **Signature**: For authorizing programs and transactions

Some other useful, Ethereum-specific facts are listed as follows:

- Like a transaction, a digital signature is required for deploying a smart contract. A deployed smart contract is permanent and is immutable.
- A smart contract is assigned an address. If a smart contract has a bug, the corrected smart contract will be deployed with a newly assigned address, and therefore it is treated as a completely new smart contract. In other words, the corrected contract has no relationship to the old one. Consequently, the history of the old smart contract gets lost.
- Unlike a full node, a light node does not store the whole distributed ledger, but it stores the parts it cares about from someone it trusts.
- Since smart contract scripts are stored at nodes worldwide, it provides an additional layer of security.
- Ethereum provides fault tolerance. As long as at least one full node survives during a catastrophic attack, the network can be rebuilt from the surviving node and grows to a full network.
- The scalability issue is one of the main criticisms of Ethereum, as all full nodes run the same smart contract code.

Summary

Blockchain is an emerging technology. Thanks to its immutability; transparency; and the consensus mechanism, along with other clever designs such as blocks chained with the hashes of the previous blocks, the technology allows untrusting parties to trade with each other. In this chapter, we explained the basic concepts of two popular public blockchain platforms—bitcoin and Ethereum. Most of the discussions were about bitcoin, which is the mother of the technology. We also talked about Ethereum in detail, which extended bitcoin and introduced the concept of smart contracts. The introduction of smart contracts makes the Ethereum platform generic and allows us to develop applications beyond bitcoin's cash payment use case. The concept of an enterprise blockchain, along with one of the examples, Hyperledger, was mentioned as well. In addition, we briefly touched on the evolution of blockchain to give readers an idea on trends in the blockchain industry.

In the next chapter, Chapter 2, *STO – Security Token Offering*, we will discuss the concepts of ICO and STO in detail.

STO - Security Token Offering 2

Chapter 1, *Introduction to Blockchain*, covered topics about blockchain technology and, specifically, the details regarding bitcoin and Ethereum. From our discussion, you should have got the idea that blockchain is a decentralized technology. Companies, government institutions, and international organizations (for example, UNICEF) are utilizing this technology to improve efficiency and lower costs.

Whenever a disruptive technology emerges, startups are commonly the pioneers in turning it into real applications and disrupting current business models. A fundamental question is how these startups are funded. Without being properly funded, there will be very few or no startups working on new projects, which will ultimately affect success or failure of the new technology. For raising funds to support blockchain startups, new funding methods, for example, **initial coin offering (ICO)** and STO, were invented and used, in addition to traditional funding methods.

In this chapter, we will first talk about traditional fund raising methods, such as angel funds, **venture capital (VC)** funds, **private equity (PE)** funds, and **initial public offering (IPO)**. At the formation stage of a startup, angel funds or seed money plays an important role. VC funds start to invest after a startup passes the formation stage. PE and other funding sources will support the company until it becomes mature enough and is ready to go for an IPO. With an ICO, a startup takes a different path.

At the formation stage, most blockchain startups bypass the private fund raising steps, and directly turns to the public for investments. STOs, the most promising alternative to ICOs, will likely support future growth of the blockchain industry after the ICO bubble burst.

Therefore, in this chapter, we will discuss ICOs and STOs in detail. More specifically, we will cover the following topics:

- A traditional fundraising roadmap for startups
- The initial coin offering
- The security token offering

A traditional fund raising roadmap for startups

Raising funds is the most critical task for any entrepreneur starting a new business venture. Many startups fail due to insufficient money to support future activities. Prior to the capitalism age, funding for a major adventure relied on support from royal or rich families. This approach could only support a small number of projects. It was hard for adventurers to find a willing sponsor. For example, Columbus sought many European royal families to support his adventure and was turned down. Eventually, Spain's King Ferdinand and Queen Isabella agreed to finance his journey. Then, capitalism came, and along with it came the concept of incorporation. This opened a door to a new way of raising capitals from investors to finance new business ventures. A famous example is the East India Company, which was created by British merchant adventurers in 1600. The company was started with the personal fortunes of the partners. The East India Company later sold company stocks to investors and became the world's first commercial corporation.

More recently, startups are a primary force that's working on new ventures. A startup is a company in its initial stages. It is created by its entrepreneurial founders to develop a product or service that they envision will be in demand. At a startup formation stage, it carries a high risk. VC funds are unwilling to invest in it. Seed money steps up to fill in a gap. A common type of seed money is angel fund. In the late 1990s and early 2000s, dotcom startups were very common. During that time, VCs were very active in investing in dotcom startups at their early stages. At their middle stages, PE firms often provided financial support. When a company becomes established with a tested business model and recurrent revenues, it often goes to the next stage of going public via an IPO. IPO helps the company to raise additional capital from the public investors in order to fund future business growth. Between PE capitals and an IPO, the mezzanine capital can provide funds to bridge a gap. The mezzanine capital is a mix of equity and debt. Its debt part provides an option for a company's owners to obtain funds without further diluting its ownership.

In summary, a traditional funding roadmap for a startup could be as follows:

- **Seed money/angel funds**: The formation stage
- **VC funds**: Early rounds of funding
- **PE firms**: Funding companies at their middle stages
- **Mezzanine capital**: Bridging to the IPO phase
- **IPO**: Selling equity stakes to the public for raising capital to support further expansions

In the rest of this section, we illustrate these funding methods.

Seed money

A newly formed startup usually doesn't have a track record. VC capitalists are often sceptical of the new venture's prospects for success and won't invest in them. Seed money becomes the best hope for the startup founders to raise their initial capitals. In return, the seed money investors receive an equity stake in the company.

Seed money, also named seed capital or seed funding, is the first round of capital that's used to fund a startup during its launch stage. Statistically, around a third of startups fail as a result of running out of cash due to the lack of adequate funding sources. Therefore, seed money plays a critically important role in a startup's initial creation and growth. The word *seed* here gives the meaning for a startup to grow, similar to planting a seed for a tree to grow. Seed money is mainly used for preliminary operations, such as setting up a startup, hiring a lawyer/accountant, employing core team members, marketing, product development, and so on.

A startup can go to the following to obtain seed money:

- **Angel investors**: These are wealthy individuals that commonly having a vision regarding the startup and where it can lead to. Therefore, they are more willing to take the risk and invest in a new venture that is no more than an idea on paper.
- **Family members and friends**: They know the startup founders personally and choose to believe in them. They are often the strongest supporters.
- Equity crowdfunding investors or accredited investors.
- **Seed VC firms**: Companies such as 500 startups, SV Angel, and Andreessen Horowitz are active seed VC firms.
- Government programs and grants.
- Money pooled from the founders' own savings and loans.
- Online crowdfunding platforms, such as SeedInvest and Seedrs. Investors make their investment decisions based on their assessments of the founders' credentials and the merits of their proposed projects.

Angel investors and angel funds

Angel capitals are a common type of seed money, which provide financial support to a new startup. Angel funds are investment funds where the money is pooled from angel investors. Angel investors are normally high net worth individuals or companies with insights on industries they invest in.

More specifically, they are also called an **angel funder**, business angel, private investor, seed investor, or informal investor. Angel investors have the following characteristics:

- Need to satisfy the **Securities and Exchange Commission (SEC)** standards for accredited investors with a net worth of $1 million or more and at least an annual income of $200,000
- Invest in small startups or entrepreneurs, who are among an entrepreneur's family members or friends
- Sometimes invest online through equity crowdfunding
- May provide advice to their invested companies
- Typically use their own money instead of pooled money from others
- Provide capital, usually in exchange for convertible debt or ownership equity
- By pooling an angel investors' money into an angel fund, a fund can invest a large sum into a project and gain better negotiating powers

VC fund

VC is invested at an early stage, in an emerging startup or small business with long-term growth potential after the new company has survived through its formation stage. VCs are normally contributed by wealthy investors, investment banks, or other financial institutions. Capital is pooled into funds called VC funds. VC funds often invest in specific areas in order to pursue preset goals. Venture capitalists manage VC funds. Hence, a VC fund is a PE investment vehicle with an objective of investing in new businesses with high risks and high returns in their early stages. In return, VC funds receive a share of the ownership in the new company. Along with financial support, VC funds can help new companies with their managerial and technical expertise.

Compared to the startups that are invested in by seed money, the risk of the ventures that are invested by a VC fund should have reduced. Another difference is the investment amount, as well as the terms of the transaction. VC funds normally invest a much larger sum of money and involve complex contract terms. On the other hand, the amount of investment capital that's raised in seed money is typically lower.

Other useful facts about VC include the following:

- Including the seed VC funds, a VC investment can be categorized into five different stages: startup stage, early stage, growth stage, late stage, and buyouts/recapitalizations stage.

- The first round of a VC investment is called Series A funding, then followed by Series B, C, D, E, and so on.
- The minimal expected return set by investors on a VC fund is 20% per year so that they are compensated for taking high risks.
- VC is often a primary or the only funding source for startups since, with no or very limited revenues, these startups do not have access to traditional capital markets such as issuing of bonds or public shares.
- Return on VC investment is materialized through an existing action, such as selling the stake at an initial public offering or a merger and acquisition of the invested company by another company.
- VC capitalists usually receive a significant portion of the company's ownership due to the large sum of money they have invested. Therefore, they gain some control over making decisions for the company. When the company has sizable and sustainable revenues, venture capitalists have the ability to appoint a new management team and push out the founding team. This possibility is a major concern to founders of startups.

Private equity firms

PE refers to the equity or shares that represent the ownership of interest in an entity that is not publicly traded or listed. PE is an alternative investment class. PE funds are generally organized as limited partnerships. A limited partnership generally consists of a general partner who manages the fund and limited partners who are passive investors. A general partner usually invests and hence owns 1% interest in a fund and assumes full liability, and is responsible for managing as well as operating the fund.

 The limited partners usually own 99% interest of the fund and only have limited liability in the fund.

PE firms raise funds from wealthy individuals, accredited investors, and institutional investors such as endowments, banks, insurance companies, and pension funds.

PE investments are managed by PE firms. PE firms charge a fee for their services provided. The fee consists of two parts, the management fee and performance fee.

 The management fee rate varies from 1.0% to 2.0% per year initially and later will be reduced by 0.5% to 1.0%. The performance fee is usually around 20% of profits from investments.

PE funds can invest in startups or private companies or in the privatization of a public company.

They finance companies at their middle and mature stages for purposes such as company growth, buyouts, and so on. Common PE investment objectives include leveraged buyouts, growth capital, distressed investments, and mezzanine capital. PE was thought by some people to be a rebranding of leveraged buyout firms post the 1980s. Big PE firms, for example, The Carlyle Group, **Kohlberg Kravis Roberts** (**KKR**), and The Blackstone Group, invest in leveraged buyout transactions in mature companies.

PE funds are often confused with angel funds or VC funds. For example, they are all private capitals investing in companies and exit by selling their stakes in equity financing, like IPOs. However, they are quite different. For instance, PE firms make investments in fewer companies but larger amounts than those made by angels and VCs. PE firms often buy 100% ownership of a company, while a VC firm likely buys 50% or less ownership.

Most VC firms diversify their risk by investing in many different startups. Consequently, the return-on-investment of PE frequently depends on one investment. Another difference is the investment timing. As we mentioned previously, PE firms buy mature/established companies and streamline their operations to increase revenues. VC firms invest in startups with high growth potential.

With the investments from PE, a company can develop new technology and products, acquire competitors, bolster its balance sheet, increase working capitals, or streamline the company's operations.

Mezzanine capital/fund

A mezzanine fund is a pool of capital to be invested in mezzanine finance. Mezzanine finance is a mix of part debt and part equity financing. They are like warrants, containing equity-based options, along with a lower-priority debt for providing flexible long-term capital for a company to achieve its business objectives. In the case of a company default, it gives the lender an option to convert into an equity stake of the company. This conversion right can only be executed after other senior lenders or investors such as VC are paid, since mezzanine capital financing is unsecured. Consequently, it usually has a higher interest rate (for example, 12% to 20%) and a higher portion of equity stake when a conversion occurs. A mezzanine capital investment period is normally five to seven years.

Mezzanine financing can be structured as debt, for example, a subordinated and unsecured note or preferred shares. Here are two examples:

- **$150m of unsecured subordinated notes with warrants**: 12% interest rate under unsecured subordinated notes or if warrants being converted into equity and 5% of the ownership of the company
- **$120m of redeemable preferred shares with warrants**: 14% interest rate on preferred shares or if being converted into equity and 6% of the ownership of the company

For a company, mezzanine financing represents a third financing option, together with a standard loan or equity fundraising. It provides a way for founders of a company to raise a portion of funds via debt-like financing without diluting their ownership of the company. A company can use this money to finance acquisitions, make company buyouts, support growth, or prepare for an IPO.

IPO

IPO refers to a private company selling stock to the public for the first time. Upon successful completion of an IPO, the company becomes public. Therefore, IPO turns a private company into a public company and is sometimes called *going public*.

There are many differences between a private company and a public company. For example, a private company has a limited number of shareholders who can be the founders, key employees, or private investors. Shares of a private company cannot be traded at a stock exchange. On the other hand, ownership of a public company is widely held by public investors, and shares can be traded at stock exchanges. To keep shareholders informed, a public company is required by SEC to publish financial statements regularly. In summary, a private company is not open to public investments while a public company is open to the market.

 A public company can go to the public markets repeatedly to raise additional funds. This fundraising event is called a **follow-on public offer**.

IPO offers a way for private shareholders to cash in their early investments. An IPO has many advantages, as well as disadvantages. They are summarized as follows.

Pros

IPO has the following advantages:

- It allows a company to access a wide pool of public investors.
- Capitals raised from IPO do not need to be paid to the investors.
- No interests are paid to shareholders. Instead, dividends are paid when a company has stable revenues and is profitable. This allows a public company to preserve cash when it is in high demand or the company is not profitable.
- It allows early private investors to sell their stakes either at IPO or later at a stock exchange. Selling a private investors' shares at a public market will not dilute the existing shareholders' ownership in the company.
- It offers a company a way to obtain low-cost working capitals.
- It increases a company's public image and awareness that benefits the company's future sales and profits.
- It is easier to recruit and retain talents via programs such as an employee stock purchase plan, and so on.
- When its stock price is highly valued, equity shares are an effective currency to make strategic acquisitions of other companies.
- It's the best option to raise the largest amount of money.
- It diversifies the shareholder base.
- It opens a door to additional fundraising strategies, for example, warrants, rights, preferred shares, bonds, and convertible debts.

Cons

IPO has the following disadvantages:

- IPO is expensive, for example, you have to pay for high banking, legal, and marketing fees. After an IPO, the company has ongoing expenses to prepare mandatory financial/regulatory reports, accounting, tax, and other business information.
- There's a risk of reducing an IPO price significantly if the company is not well perceived by the public investors.
- The dissemination of information to the public may put the company at a disadvantage to its competitors.
- It may be more difficult for founders to control the company effectively due to diluted ownership.

- It's open to legal issues such as lawsuits from shareholders or government agencies.

An IPO is usually underwritten by one or a syndicate of investment banks. The investment banks work with founders or a management team throughout the process of the IPO. For instance, the investment banks prepare roadshows, set up a target price range, build a book, arrange for the shares to be listed at one or more stock exchanges, and so on.

More specifically, a typical IPO process may include the following steps:

1. Present a plan to the board of directors to gain an approval
2. Appoint a task force team
3. Prepare and review financial information about the company
4. Send letters of intent to prospective investment banks and select a lead underwriter
5. Draft the preliminary prospectus, that is, a business statement describing the company and prepared for potential investors
6. Underwriters complete a detailed due diligence investigation of the company
7. Present the company profile and preliminary prospectus to SEC for registration and review
8. Assemble a syndicate of investment banks for accessing and selling shares to a larger pool of potential investors
9. Start roadshows by having meetings with potential investors and analysts
10. Underwriters build the book by collecting names of investors and the number of shares
11. Decide on the offering size and set up a target price range
12. On the IPO day, the syndicate of investment banks set up a primary market, allocate their shares to investors proportionally based on the book, and start trading shares at the secondary stock exchanges afterward.

The initial coin offering

In the previous section, we talked about a traditional fundraising roadmap for blockchain startups. However, startup founders do have concerns regarding private investors such as VC capitalists. It is possible that VC capitalists establish their own management team and push out the founders when the company is on a solid footing.

Internet and blockchain provide technical platforms for entrepreneurs who can reach out directly to public investors for raising funds. Consequently, ICOs became the most popular fundraising methods for founders to finance their blockchain projects. ICOs give blockchain startup founders a way to bypass IPOs and raise a large sum of money from public investors at the startup formation stage. In 2017 and 2018, tens of billions of USD were raised via ICOs. Since ICOs are closely related to tokens and crowdfunding, we will first explain the basic concepts of tokens and crowdfunding.

Coins and tokens

When we talk about blockchain and cryptocurrency, many people use coin and token interchangeably and treat them as synonyms. In fact, they are not necessarily identical. There are differences between them.

A currency is required to have three functions:

- **Circulation as a medium of exchange**: Units of the currency paid by a buyer to a seller in exchange for goods or services from the seller
- **Unit of account**: Value of goods or services can be measured by a currency
- **Store of value**: Being treated as an asset that can be saved, retrieved, and exchanged in the future for other assets or goods and services

The US dollar is an example of a currency that incorporates the preceding three functions. A currency that's issued by a central bank of a country often has both paper bills with different denominations (for example, $1, $2, $5, $10, $20, $50, and $100 bills for USD) and metal coins (for example, penny, nickel, dime, quarter, dollar, and so on). Cryptocurrency is a digital form of currency. Bitcoin satisfies all three functions of a currency and exists only digitally. Therefore, it is a cryptocurrency.

Blockchain coins are created using encryption techniques and store value over time. Coins are used for circulation and can pay for goods and services, as long as a seller accepts them. In other words, it is correct to refer to coins as cryptocurrencies. Hence, the term coin refers to digital money. Besides bitcoin, other well-known coins are Ripple, Ether, and EOS. Coins share similar characteristics as money. For example, they are fungible, divisible, portable, and durable. The maximum number of coins to be minted is fixed at the time when a coin is initially launched.

Some coins are issued based on the original protocol proposed by Satoshi Nakamoto, such as bitcoin, bitcoin cash, and bitcoin SV. Other coins are issued following a new protocol that is derived and enhanced from the original protocol, for example, Ether and Ripple. Coins exist on public blockchain platforms only. Private blockchain usually doesn't involve a coin.

Tokens are digital assets that are created for a project. They are used as a way to facilitate payments within the project's ecosystem. In this ecosystem, the project-specific tokens play a similar role to coins.

Tokens can be further categorized into security tokens and utility tokens. Security tokens give holders a share of a company's ownership, for example, tokens issued by the **Decentralized Autonomous Organization** (**DAO**) project. Utility tokens give holders access to the product or service on the blockchain platform.

Tokens issued by following Ethereum ERC-20 token standards are examples of tokens. Tokens are not intended for circulation. Outside its intended project, tokens cannot be used to pay for goods and services. Therefore, tokens should not be treated as cryptocurrencies.

Another difference between coins and tokens is how they are implemented technically. Usually, significant effort is required to write new code in order to issue a new type of coin (cryptocurrency). Ether and EOS are coins that were issued on the Ethereum and EOS blockchain platforms, respectively.

Creating a token is a lot easier. For example, Ethereum ERC-20 tokens can be issued by supplying mandatory parameters, for example, the token name and the total number of tokens, to a template. This involves very minor coding and requires only a few steps to complete. ERC-20 tokens that are created for different projects on Ethereum can be converted into each other and use the same wallet.

In summary, the main differences between coins and tokens are as follows:

- Coins are a way of payment, whereas tokens can represent a share of a company's stake or provide access to a product or service on the platform.
- Coins are cryptocurrencies that can be used like a currency to buy or sell goods and services. You can use a coin to purchase a token, but you can't use a token to buy a coin.
- Coins can operate independently of a project's ecosystem, whereas tokens have a specific usage within the project's ecosystem only.

Crowdfunding

Crowdfunding is a way of raising many small amounts of money from a large pool of investors to fund a project or business venture. Investors can be friends, family members, customers, individual investors, and so on. For better exposure to supporters, crowdfunding is typically hosted on the internet, crowdfunding platforms, or on social media sites. Because of this, the term crowdfunding represents internet-mediated registries.

The concept of crowdfunding has been around for centuries with a long history. However, to many, especially for people outside the US, it is a new and alternative way of raising funds. Several driving forces made crowdfunding popular and well-known in this century:

- The wide adoption of the internet and social media sites
- More crowdfunding sites such as Kiva, Indiegogo, GoFundMe (2010), YouCaring, and RocketHub started to serve these needs
- **Jumpstart Our Business startups Act (JOBS)**, signed by President Barack Obama on April 5, 2012, includes provisions that allow for crowdfunding
- **Regulation Crowdfunding (Reg CF)**, starting on May 16, 2016, allows a startup to raise up to $1,070,000 USD in a 12 month period
- The majority of ICOs were held in the form of crowdfunding

It is estimated that, in 2015, over $34 billion USD was raised via crowdfunding worldwide. Money that's been raised via crowdfunding has been used to finance ventures such as technology, artistic, medical expenses, travel, or community/social projects.

Crowdfunding involves three groups of players:

- Project initiators who recommend the project
- Groups of supporters that provide a small sum each
- A platform or moderating organization that matches initiators and supporters

There are two primary types of crowdfunding:

- **Rewards crowdfunding**: Initiators pre-sell a product or service to supporters without incurring debt or giving out equity shares
- **Equity crowdfunding**: Initiators give out equity shares to supporters in exchange for a sum of money

A crowdfunding-based ICO belongs to rewards crowdfunding, while STO, which will be discussed in detail later, belongs to the second type, equity crowdfunding.

ICO and its difference to IPO

In ICO, the word coin can mean a coin or a token. When a proposed blockchain project is to create a new cryptocurrency, coin will refer to a coin. If the new project is to build a platform for a product or service, then coin refers to a utility token. Many people do not separate the two cases and refer to both as utility tokens.

Most of ICOs are completed either via a crowdfunding event or via a private ICO. Before working on raising funds from an ICO, the founders of a blockchain startup write a document called a white paper describing the idea, the business plan, and the project. The paper will also explain the following:

- The amount of money needed to complete the project
- What cryptocurrencies and fiat currencies are acceptable
- What type of tokens are issued
- How many tokens are issued
- The duration of the ICO

Let's use a hypothetical blockchain project to explain how an ICO works. Suppose you are a motivated entrepreneur who plans to build a blockchain platform for facilitating private tutoring on university courses. This platform will match parties of tutors and students to enter a transaction. Here, a transaction refers to a student paying a tutor for providing the tutoring service. To raise money for financing the education project, you turn to ICO for raising capitals by issuing utility tokens called **EduCoin**. You will first set up an attractive website and write an appealing white paper to promote your ideas. You will then choose to either hold a public crowdfunding ICO, which is more common, or a private ICO, which is less common.

Let's assume you take the crowdfunding approach. On the internet, you will ask your potential supporters or investors to send you digital coins, for example, BTC and Ether, or fiat currency such as USD. In return, you send them EduCoin tokens based on a predefined valuation formula. The pre-sold EduCoin tokens are a small portion of all tokens, say 5%. Holders of these tokens can receive tutoring services in the future after you have successfully built your tutoring blockchain platform. The holders, however, do not own a share of ownership in your company. If you receive digital coins, you will sell them at a cryptocurrency exchange such as Binance or OKEx to convert them into fiat currency. You can then invest the money into the project. For investors, they hope your project becomes successful and the EduCoin tokens can be used. Consequently, the value of the token increases. Investors can then cash in their investments for a profit.

If the total money from an ICO fails to meet the minimum amount required for the project, the money that's raised will be returned to the investors. The ICO is declared to be unsuccessful. Otherwise, the money that's raised will be used in the project until it's completed or the money has been used up.

In July 2013, Mastercoin held their first ICO. Ethereum held its ICO in 2014 and raised 3,700 BTC, an equivalent of $2.1 million dollars (based on the BTC price at the time) during the first 12 hours. In 2017 and 2018, ICO became a very popular fundraising method. ICOs help to raise large sums of money.

This is eye-popping as, at the time when an ICO takes place, a startup does not have a concrete product. Its only product is an idea in a white paper! If any of the blockchain startups had followed a traditional funding approach such as raising capitals from an angel fund or a seed VC fund, the startup would be lucky to raise a small fraction of that from its ICO.

Blockchain startups have heavily relied on ICOs. ICOs skip the early fundraising steps and disrupt IPOs, which are heavily regulated and rigorously monitored. The lack of regulation and monitoring puts investors at risk of losing their investments. Before we proceed to a discussion about the issues with ICO, we will first talk about the differences between ICOs and IPOs:

- IPOs involve investment banks to provide essential services, such as matching founders with investors, conducting due diligence reviews, building the demand book, allocating shares, and arranging to list the new stock. Investment banks are paid handsomely, commonly with a percentage of the planned IPO size, for the service that's provided. ICOs do not involve an intermediary such as investment banks. An ICO site matches the founders with the public investors directly. In other words, ICOs are like decentralized IPOs. This method keeps the costs of raising capitals low. However, without the due diligence review and verification by a third party such as an investment bank, investors face a high risk.
- IPOs need to be registered with a regulatory agency, for example, in US with SEC, and are heavily regulated. ICOs are not regulated, leaving a door open to scams.
- Due to regulation and steps on verification, an IPO takes a longer time, for example, up to six months. An ICO takes a shorter time to complete, for example, up to one month.
- The IPO requires a company to file financial and regulatory reports after an IPO. An ICO does not require a startup to publish financial reports. Therefore, after receiving an offer, the costs of running these companies are different.

- The stock of an IPO company are traded at regulated stock exchange markets such as **New York Stock Exchange** (**NYSE**) or Nasdaq. The coins of an ICO startup are traded at unregulated cryptocurrency exchanges.
- Shares from an IPO represent ownership in the company. Tokens from an ICO gives investors access to a future product or service that's yet to be developed, not ownership of the ICO issuer.
- IPOs have high barriers for companies to enter. For example, a company has to satisfy certain financial and business requirements, such as a track record of earnings, stable cash flows, recurring revenues, and equity assets. ICOs almost have no barriers. All that's required is for founders to write a white paper detailing a new idea that is appealing to potential supporters and investors.
- IPOs are heavy in providing legal documents, for example, preparing a prospectus. ICOs do not have such a requirement. Founders can even start an ICO with a deck of PowerPoint slides.
- IPOs are usually targeted at institutional investors. Ordinary investors cannot access IPOs. ICOs are open to everybody.

The ICO bubble

After the first ICO in July 2013, ICOs have quickly become a primary fundraising method for financing blockchain projects. Since 2014, blockchain startups have raised tens of billions of USD via ICOs. Reports on the total amounts that were raised via ICOs are not consistent. Many websites collect statistics on ICOs. We use data from `https://www.icodata.io/`, which claims to be the world's biggest and most accurate ICO database, for our discussions.

With data from ICODATA.IO, the yearly total number of ICOs and amounts that were raised between 2014 and 2018 are listed in the following table:

Year	Number of ICOs	Total amount raised in USD
2014	2	16,032,802
2015	3	6,084,000
2016	29	90,250,273
2017	876	6,226,689,449
2018	1,251	7,705,825,063

The preceding table shows ICOs taking off in 2016 and reaching their peak in 2017 and 2018. However, the yearly figures are not revealing enough. We need to turn to the monthly graphs (taken from the ICODATA.IO website under the **Stats** heading) of ICO amounts.

The following graph shows the monthly ICO amounts for 2017:

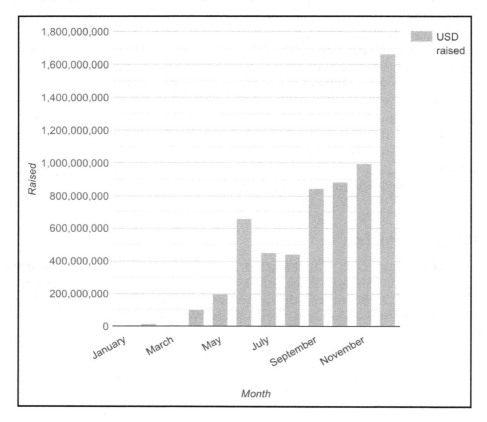

The following graph shows the monthly ICO amounts for 2018:

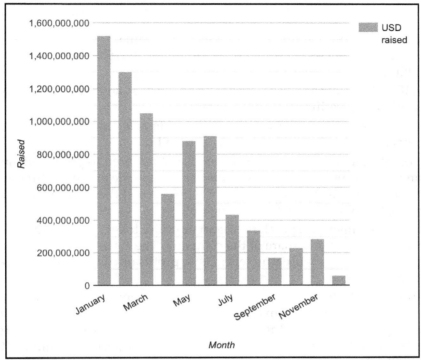

These graphs show that ICO activities reached to a hectic level in late 2017 and early 2018, and then retreated dramatically in the second half of 2018. The most updated figure from ICODATA.IO for January 2019 (as of January 27) is $3.6 m. This is back to the level it reached in January 2017, which is $14 m. Essentially, an ICO bubble has formed and burst within two years.

The gold rush leading to the ICO bubble can be exemplified by one example. In May 2017, a web browser called Brave completed an ICO by raising $36 m, which is the equivalent of ETH (156,250 Ethers) within the first 25 seconds!

The hyper on ICOs is a primary driving force behind a roller coaster path of the cryptocurrency values during 2017 – 2018. One main reason that led to the burst of the ICO bubble is a high failure rate in ICO funded blockchain projects. Less than half of ICOs have survived over four months after the offering, and near half (around 46%) of ICOs that took place in 2017 failed by February 2018. Consequently, ICO investors, who invested late, have suffered heavy losses. In many cases, they lost all their investments.

ICOs provide an innovative fundraising method that allows people worldwide to invest in groundbreaking blockchain projects. What went terribly wrong with ICO that lead to its dramatic downfall? Here, we list some thoughts on possible reasons:

- An ICO does not require registration with a regulatory agency such as SEC. Regulation agencies do not have the necessary information to regulate and monitor ICOs.
- An ICO does not involve an intermediary such as an investment bank to conduct due diligence verification on the company.
- An ICO does not require a startup to provide detailed documentation such as the prospectus describing the company in detail.
- Upon completion of an ICO, a startup is not required to provide financial statements as well as business updates to the public investors. Investors cannot effectively monitor the progress of the project that they have invested in. Investors also do not know how their money was used.
- Via an ICO, investors purchase a coin or utility token, which is not tied to a real underlying asset or a share of the company. The coins or tokens become worthless if the proposed project fails or profits or coins are not delivered as being promised.
- Early stage startups are not suitable to ordinary investors, who lack the skills and resources to make good investment decisions. This is a reason why, under security laws, only wealthy sophisticated investors (for example, accredited investors and angel investors), professional investors (for example, VC capitalists) or institutional investors (for example, pension funds and banks) are allowed to invest in IPOs and high risk startups. ICOs that allow ordinary investors to participate in such investments bypasses the well-tested rules in security laws.
- ICO issued coins are to be traded at cryptocurrency exchanges, which are also not regulated. This opens a door to trading practices that violate security laws, for example, front running and painting the tape (also called washed trades). Front running refers to make a trade ahead of a client by utilizing knowledge on the client's trade for a profit. Painting the tape refers to a group of investors trading among themselves to generate an illusion of liquidity on a security.
- **Know Your Customer** (**KYC**) and **Anti-Money Laundering** (**AML**) are not required for ICOs. This potentially makes ICOs an ideal tool for engaging illegal activities such as money laundering.
- No thorough background checks on founders are conducted and revealed.

In summary, the ICO fundraising method lacks proper control. They are open to scams and fraud. SEC has alerted investors about pump and dump schemes in ICOs. In such a scam, scammers inflate the value of an ICO for generating interest and driving up the price of the coins. They then quickly sell the coins to lock in a profit. The UK **Financial Conduct Authority (FCA)** has also issued warnings on ICO scams. The **European Securities and Markets Authority (ESMA)** pointed out the high risks associated with ICOs and warned that investors could lose all of their money. China and South Korea have completely banned ICOs.

In addition, SEC has started to crack down on fraudulent and non-compliant ICOs. For example, on December 11, 2017, SEC issued an order against an ICO initiator, Munchee Inc., and declared it to be a fraudulent ICO. SEC also work on setting and enforcing standards in the industry. We will explain this in more detail in `Chapter 3`, *Monetizing Digital Tokens Under US Security Laws*. Social media sites such as Twitter, Google, and Mailchimp have banned advertisements of ICOs on their sites. Other sites such as Facebook, Snapchat, and LinkedIn puts restrictions on startups from promoting ICOs. Internet sites in China such as Baidu, Tencent, and Weibo have also banned ICO marketing. Similar actions were taken by the Japanese site, Line, and the Russian site, Yandex.

Early investors were rewarded handsomely in late 2017 as cryptocurrency prices reaching unprecedented high levels. Being encouraged by the high rewards, new investors chose to ignore these issues. As the prices of main cryptocurrencies such as BTC, ether, and XRP tanked, many investors suffered heavy losses. With their lesson learned from ICOs, the blockchain community now turns to STOs for addressing the non-control issue that's faced by ICOs and support the blockchain industry's future growth.

The STO

STOs are emerging to be the new way of crowdfunding since they offer investors with the governance and protection that isn't provided by ICOs. A Toronto-based company, Node Blockchain Inc., has published a recent study (`https://drive.google.com/file/d/1Kuwu0bWR8Mk5TOErJ1QNBbM3bLj0T6_p/view`) supporting the idea of STOs being the future fundraising methods to support the growth of the blockchain industry.

An ICO issues either a coin (cryptocurrency) or utility token. STO issues a security token, which is a digital stock certificate. It is different from a utility token. A utility token is treated to be a commodity, like gold with a useful value, but isn't used for security. To compare STOs and ICOs in detail, we need to explore the concept of security first.

Security

A security is a tradable financial asset. The legal definition of a security varies by countries. In some countries, a security includes equities and fixed income instruments. In some other countries, hybrid instruments such as convertibles, equity warrants, and so on are included in the definition of a security. In the US, commonly known securities include debt securities such as commercial papers; bonds and debentures; equity securities such as stocks; or a more exotic type, derivatives, such as forwards, futures, options, and swaps. We will explain the definition of security and how to determine whether a coin is a security under the US securities law in the next chapter. In the UK, securities, as outlined by FCA, include equities, debentures, alternative debentures, and units, along with stakeholder or personal pension schemes.

Securities are different from commodities. For example, equity securities represent ownership of a company, while commodities are items of useful value, but are not considered as a right to ownership. Securities can only be traded at registered trading platforms and participants that trade securities are required to be registered broker and dealers under the applicable securities laws. Commodity or currencies trading platforms for spot markets don't need to be licensed. For instance, cryptocurrency exchanges are not regulated and do not need to be licensed. In the US, the **Commodity Futures Trading Commission (CFTC)** defines bitcoin to be a commodity and the **Internal Revenue Service (IRS)** defines cryptocurrency as property. SEC views many ICO issued tokens to be securities, which the blockchain community has a different view. For example, in July 2017, SEC declared the DAO token to be a security.

In the real word, the definition of a security is far more complicated. For instance, an e-money or payment service can be considered a security. Normally, a country's security regulatory agency publishes guidelines to define what qualifies as a security.

In the US, the Supreme Court has created the Howey Test to determine whether a transaction is an investment contract. Under the Howey test, you have to ask the following four questions:

- Whether it is an investment of money
- Whether it is expecting profits from the investment
- Whether it is an investment of money in a common enterprise
- Whether there is any profit from the efforts of a promoter or third party

If the answer is yes, a token sale is considered to be a security that's subject to securities laws.

Any business that's involved in tradable financial assets (securities) is required to comply with laws for financial services and consumer protection. Two well-known laws are the **Bank Secrecy Act** (**BSA**) and the USA Patriot Act.

BSA, which was signed into law on October 26, 1970 by President Richard Nixon, requires businesses to do the following:

- Maintain records of cash transactions of negotiable instruments
- File reports if the total transactions in a day exceed $10,000
- Report suspicious activities, which may imply money laundering, tax evasion, or other criminal activities

BSA is also referred to as the Currency and Foreign Transactions Reporting Act and is more often called an AML law.

The USA Patriot Act, which was signed into law on October 26, 2001 by President George W. Bush, is passed by congress to strengthen national security in response to the September 11 terrorist attacks in 2001. The act has ten titles. The third title is called anti-money-laundering to prevent terrorism, modifying parts of BSA and the **Money Laundering Control Act** (**MLCA**) of 1986 to prevent terrorism.

Pursuant to the USA Patriot Act, the US government issued regulations, making KYC mandatory for US financial institutions. Any businesses that conduct security transactions need to follow regulations on KYC as well. KYC stands for know your customer or know your client. KYC is the process in which businesses collect and verify information about the identity and address of their customers. Companies use this information to ensure that their services are not misused for illegal activities such as money laundering, criminal activities, or bribery. The KYC procedure is required to be completed by companies while opening customer accounts. Post an account opening, the process also needs to be followed periodically.

STO verses ICO

The biggest difference between STOs and ICOs is that STOs issue a token that is considered to be a security, whereas ICOs issue a token (or coin) that can be a utility, commodity (or currency), or a security. This could result in many differences in the offering processes.

Regulatory risk: SEC may view an ICO as an issuance of a security and take actions against fundraisers, including canceling ICOs and returning raised funds to the original investors. STOs, if done properly and compliant to security laws, will not have such a risk. The following are examples of the reasons:

- **Requirements on AML and KYC**: STOs have to follow the AML and KYC laws or regulations and ICOs do not have such obligations.
- **Requirements on securities laws**: STO issued tokens need to follow the relevant securities laws and ICO issued tokens do not need to follow.
- **Intermediaries involvement**: The ICO process does not require services provided by bankers, lawyers, or any other intermediaries. The STO process involves these intermediaries. Some recent studies show that the involvement of intermediaries and middleman entities help to improve and create efficiencies.
- **Ideology**: The STO fundraising approach moved away from the decentralized ideology (for example, still having intermediary involvement) that is a core idea in blockchain industry, whereas ICOs follow the idea of decentralization.
- **Secondary trading markets**: ICOs issued coins are traded at cryptocurrency exchanges that do not need to obtain licenses, whereas STO issued tokens have to trade at licensed exchanges via registered broker-dealers at higher costs because of the required supervision and employment of licensed staff.
- **Governance and control**: An STO process provides a governance and control framework that makes scams and fraud much less likely, whereas an ICO lacks sufficient control, which can lead to many scams.
- **Documentation**: STOs need to comply with applicable securities laws since it issues a security, whereas ICOs do not need to comply with applicable securities laws and instead just need to provide (at most) a white paper.
- **Cost/duration**: STOs are more expensive and take a longer time to complete the process of registration with the securities regulatory authority and comply with the securities and other regulatory rules for issuing a security, whereas ICOs do not need to follow such processes. This leads to lower costs as well as a shorter duration to complete an ICO.

Security token issuers are subject to other constraints, which we will discuss later. These limitations are time-consuming, intrusive, and expensive.

STO versus IPO

Both STOs and IPOs issue new securities, and therefore adhere to securities laws. Both need to follow AML as well as KYC. They differ in several key areas.

An IPO process is time- and resource-consuming. The JOBS Act, signed into law on April 5, 2012 by President Barack Obama, permits startups and small businesses to be able to raise capital from the public without going through the lengthy IPO process. Title III of the JOBS Act, also called the CROWDFUND Act, defines a method for companies to issue securities via crowdfunding, which was not permitted before. In essence, the JOBS Act modified the Security Act of 1933 and eases securities regulations to make fundraising easier for startups and small businesses.

Although the JOBS Act was not created especially for the blockchain and cryptocurrency industries, the STO process utilizes the act for obtaining an exemption from IPO to issue a security token. This significantly reduces STOs duration and costs. Currently, security token issuers in the US can apply for one of three exemptions: Reg D, Reg A+, and Reg CF. They differ in the following places:

- The annual offer limit
- General soliciting
- Investor requirements
- SEC filing requirements
- Restriction on resales
- Preemption of state registration

Chapter 3, *Monetizing Digital Tokens Under US Security Laws*, discusses the applicable STO laws and regulations in detail.

Other differences between STOs and IPOs are summarized as follows:

- IPOs are restricted to institutional investors. Often, an IPO is a local event in a country. Accessing foreign investors can only be afforded by established companies due to the associated costs and risks. Some jumbo and high impact IPOs such as the Alibaba listing on NYSE on September 18, 2014 may attract global investors but are limited in scope. A foreign investor needs to have a broker account at the country when an IPO takes place, which is not necessarily easy to achieve. STOs provide an easy way of reaching an individual, as well as institutional investors globally, thanks to crowdfunding. In other words, STOs are not limited by geographic borders and are open to more investors over the internet, regardless of the size of a company. Past examples of ICOs that have raised tens of millions of USD within the first minute testify the advantage of reaching out to a global pool of investors. Reaching out to global investors will lead to greater secondary market liquidity post STO.

- With an IPO, a security issuer does not work with investors directly. Instead, between them, there are multiple layers of middlemen. For example, at one side, the issuer works with the underwriters (investment banks), who in turn work with global broker-dealers to attract investors. On the other hand, an investor works with a local bank, who then interacts with a broker-dealer to participate in the offering. The STO process still involves intermediaries such as lawyers. However, a security token issuer directly interacts with investors on an STO offering platform.
- IPOs are suitable for established companies normally with recurrent revenues and tested business models. These companies present smaller risks to investors. As a result, IPOs attracts high quality institutional investors. For example, by law, certain institutional investors such as insurance companies are restricted from investing in securities with high risks. They may not be qualified to invest in STOs.
- Compared to IPOs, STO issuers pay far less to investment banks and broker-dealers. Since the majority fees of an IPO go to underwriters, the overall costs of STOs are much lower than those of IPOs.
- Security tokens are created with smart contracts. Compliance that's relevant to STOs can be programmed and enforced in code. For example, rules such as transfer restrictions and security lock-up period can be programmed into the security token. That will make STO and post STO administration faster, cheaper, easier, and more robust. IPOs do not have this advantage.
- Security tokens allow for fractional ownership, just like a BTC can be split into fractions. IPO issued security has the smallest unit, one share, which cannot be divided further.

Challenges of STOs

STOs have a lot of potential. It is quickly becoming the best hope for replacing ICOs to drive the blockchain industry's future growth. On the other hand, STOs face challenges as well.

Where to trade a security token is one of these challenges. Cryptocurrency has established secondary markets for providing liquidity post ICOs. For example, as of Jan 20, 2019, `https://coinmarketcap.com/` showed that there are over 16,312 cryptocurrency markets. Secondary markets for trading STOs security tokens are scarce. So far, there are only a few reports on new security token trading platforms going live.

For example, `https://www.overstock.com/` has recently announced that its tZERO security token trading platform would go live by the end of January 2019. An STO trading platform can be a newly built trading venue on an existing **Alternative Trading System (ATS)** or on top of a cryptocurrency market. For example, Binance, the largest cryptocurrency exchange by volume, is teaming up with some stock exchanges to enable security token trading. The lack of sufficient security token trading platforms will affect a security tokens' liquidity. In turn, it negatively affects the efforts in attracting investors.

Where to register an STO is another challenge. For issuing a security token, an issuer needs to file the offering with a regulatory agency somewhere, which implies that the issuer is subject to that country's securities laws, such as AML/KYC, and regulations. When security tokens are issued globally, the corresponding STO needs to be filed with the security agencies of related countries. If security laws and regulations contradict to each other, the question is how to resolve their differences.

Similarly, these countries' securities and exchange laws progress over time. It is nearly impossible for an STO trading platform to service clients on a global scale. Even if this were possible, the associated costs and efforts could be very high. Consequently, it may not make business sense to maintain a global security token trading venue. Solutions need to be worked out in order to support a security tokens' borderless characteristics.

A third challenge is the loss of decentralization. When an issuer files with a regulatory agency, the offering process is no longer decentralized. The government agency has control over the offering process, the security token, the company, and the project. The startup has to follow the relevant laws and rules in that country. This will make blockchain decentralization enthusiasts less in favor of STOs.

Whether STOs are supported by a government is an additional challenge on this list. In the US, SEC is taking supportive steps in accommodating fundraising methods such as STO since the regulation agency views the blockchain industry positively. However, many other countries have not taken the same stand. Some countries view STO less favorably. For example, in December 2018, the PRC government officially confirmed that STOs are illegal in China.

Summary

In this chapter, we discussed a traditional fundraising roadmap for a startup. At its formation stage, seed money and angel funds are often tapped to support activities such as ideation, the creation of a company, and the development of a **Minimal Viable Product** (**MVP**). VC funds will usually invest in the startup to finance the work after an MVP is formed. PE funds will invest in a startup (company) that reaches its growth or later stage and will most likely have an established business model so that they can seek additional working capitals. IPO is the step for turning a privately held company into a public company by listing its equity securities at stock exchanges. Mezzanine capitals bridge funds before an IPO takes place.

We then discussed ICOs, which is a primarily crowdfunding-based fundraising method. ICOs became the default choice by many blockchain startups thanks to its many advantages. For example, ICOs are fast and cheaper and can reach public investors globally. We then listed the issues that are faced by ICOs and the recent downfall of ICOs.

STO was then introduced as a promising replacement to ICO in the attempt to address the shortcomings of an ICO. We explained in detail about the concept of security in order to differentiate between a utility token that's issued via an ICO and a security token issued via STO. We discussed the differences between an IPO and an STO. We ended the discussion by pointing out a few STO challenges.

The next chapter, Chapter 3, *Monetizing Digital Tokens Under US Security Laws*, will discuss an overview of applicable US security regulations on fundraising and the application of such regulations on registration and exemptions, such as Regulation D, Regulation A+, and Regulation CF, to STO in detail, along with the development of US security laws in blockchain/digital security tokens.

3
Monetizing Digital Tokens Under US Security Laws

In Chapter 2, *STO – Security Token Offering*, we covered traditional fundraising methods such as angel funds, **venture capital** (**VC**) investors, private equity funds, and **initial public offering** (**IPO**). We briefly discussed the general financing cycle from the seed round at the formation stage of a start up to the IPO. We compared this financing process to an **initial coin offering** (**ICO**), which takes a different path. For an ICO, at the formation stage, a startup bypasses the private fundraising steps—and directly turns to the public for investments.

Security token offerings (**STOs**), the most promising alternative to ICOs, will likely support future growth of the blockchain industry after the ICO bubble bursts. Therefore, in this chapter, we will discuss STOs from the legal perspective in detail.

More specifically, we will cover the following topics:

- What is an STO under US securities law?
- An overview of applicable US securities laws.
- Federal and state regulations.
- US securities law development in blockchain/digital cryptos with some real US cases.
- The process of an STO launch and legal considerations.

While there are many other issues related to STOs, we will mainly focus on the US securities law issues in this chapter.

What is an STO?

A security, in a general sense (but not according to the legal definition), is described as a financial instrument secured by a certain type of valuable asset. Securities can also be backed by revenues or profits in a company. Historically, a security is issued and purchased by signing the transaction documents on paper, such as share-purchase agreements or subscription agreements. The offer and sale of any security by any issuer in the US is subject to the federal and state securities laws and regulations.

A security token (a token classified as a security) performs a similar function as a traditional security, except that it confirms ownership through blockchain transactions rather than paper documents. Security tokens provide some key financial rights to the investors that include shares of revenue, shares of profit, equity, dividends, rights to vote, and some other financial stakes.

When an issuer issues a token that is backed by stocks, bonds, and managed real-estate trusts to purchasers with a potential return or increase in values of such tokens based on the ownership of the digital tokens, it would likely be considered as an offer or sale of securities that is subject to the US federal and state securities laws and regulations.

For an issuance of a digital token to be considered an STO, first we need to categorize it as an offer and sale of security. Hence, the question is what kind of digital token is considered as a security and hence subject to the US federal and state securities laws and regulations?

According to CoinMarketCap (https://coinmarketcap.com/), there are more than 2,000 (to be specific, 2,092) different cryptocurrencies on the market. The total market cap is $130,024,960,166 (around $130 billion—last updated: February 27, 2019 5:40 am, UTC).

There are also many other types of digital tokens that are not listed on the website.

Some possible categorizations of a digital token are as follows:

- Utility token (for example, FunFair, Timicoin)
- Virtual currency cryptocurrencies (for example, virtual coins)
- Commodity (for example, Bitcoin)
- Security—provided in the real cases in this chapter

With all these different features of digital tokens, how do we know whether a token is a security token? To answer this question, we need to have an overview of the US securities laws and know what will be covered under such laws. This will be the focus of this chapter.

Overview of US securities laws

Before getting into the analysis of how an STO would be subject to the US securities regulations under the **Securities and Exchange Commission's (SEC's)** radar, first let's look at an overview of the US securities laws that govern securities offered or sold in the US.

The first issue is jurisdiction—whether the offer and sale of security is subject to regulation in the US.

For an issuance of security to be subject to US federal and state securities, such issuance should be targeted toward potential US purchasers. Hence, for an STO to be regulated under US securities laws, the STO should be exposed to public or targeted purchasers in the US.

The offer and sale of securities in the US are regulated under both federal and state laws. In some types of offerings, the federal laws will preempt the state laws. For other types of offerings, the issuers have to satisfy both federal and state laws.

Federal regulations

In this section, we will cover some important federal regulations in the blockchain space.

Section 5 of the Securities Act of 1933

The federal securities law governing the offer and sale of a security is covered under the Securities Act of 1933, (the Securities Act). The purpose of the Securities Act is to protect the general public from making investments in fraudulent schemes. The Securities Act requires the disclosure of information that will be significant for the investors to make investment decisions. This is the main reason that the SEC requires issuers that offer and sell securities in the US to file registrations of such offerings.

Under Section 5 of the Securities Act, generally, an offer or sale of a security in the United States needs to be either registered with the SEC or exempted under one of the exemptions. However, registration of the securities offerings with the SEC is time-consuming and expensive; hence, many issuers seek ways to offer securities without the need to register. There are several ways for the offer and sale of securities in the US to be exempt from the registration requirements.

Section 3(b)(1) and (2) / Regulation A/A+ offerings (Mini IPOs)

For an STO, where the token is considered as a security and the STO does not fall squarely into any of the exemptions under the Securities Act, the issuer may consider issuing such a digital token under a Regulation A/A+ offering, which is usually referred to as a **mini IPO**.

The **Jumpstart Our Business Startups Act** (**JOBS Act**) in 2012 modified the original Regulation A (the so-called Regulation A+) and modified the Securities Act by adding Section 3(b) (2) to the Securities Act.

Like the former Regulation A, the amended Regulation A (Regulation A+) provides for mini IPOs, which are exempt from SEC registration; however, the amended Regulation A covers public offerings, where general solicitation and advertising are allowed. To offer securities under the amended Regulation A, an issuer must file an offering statement on Form 1-A (http://tinyurl.com/y69t5u7r) with the SEC, with an **offering circular** (**OC**) for distribution to investors and all required exhibits.

Form 1-A filings are subject to SEC review and comment. Before sales of securities tokens can be made, this filing and review process must evaluate the qualification of Form 1-A. This is similar to a registration statement (https://tinyurl.com/y4w4c9pr) for a registered offering to become effective. Subject to certain conditions, an issuer is allowed to test the waters or communicate with potential investors to see whether they might be interested in an offering before filing in Form 1-A; however, certain issuers under Regulation A+ are subject to ongoing reporting.

Securities sold in Regulation A+ offerings are not restricted securities (https://tinyurl.com/y3omdnvt), which means that they generally can be freely resold by nonaffiliates (https://tinyurl.com/y2onszuk) of the issuer. Certain Regulation A+ offerings benefit from federal preemption of the registration and qualification requirements of state securities laws.

Under Regulation A+, there are two tiers of offers, as described in the following list:

- **Tier-1 offer requirements**: This is an exemption for offerings of up to an aggregate total amount of $20 million in a 12-month period, which includes up to $6 million of secondary sales by the issuer's affiliates. Tier-1 securities offerings are not securities that are covered under preemptive federal exemption, but they are generally subject to state bluesky registration and qualification requirements. Tier-1 issuers are subject to minimal continuous reporting requirements.

- **Tier-2 offer requirements**: This is an exemption for offerings of up to an aggregate total amount of $50 million in a 12-month period, which includes up to $15 million of secondary sales by the issuer's affiliates. Investors in Tier-2 offerings that are not accredited investors (http://tinyurl.com/y39g8fjb) are subject to limits on the amount they may invest in a Regulation A offering. Tier-2 offerings are exempt from state bluesky registration and qualification requirements. Tier-2 issuers are subject to ongoing periodic reporting requirements.

Exemptions to Section 5 of Securities Act of 1933

The Securities Act protects the general public against fraud when they make investments in securities; however, the law carves out certain offerings from the registration requirements if such offerings are targeted at certain types of investors who the SEC considers to have the ability to appreciate the risks in the investment market and have sufficient assets to bear the risks.

Section 4(a)(2) / Reg D – Rule 506(b) and (c) – private placement exemption

Section 4(a)(2) provides a private placement exemption that mainly states that if the offering for the sale of securities is not made toward the general public, but is targeted toward some specific type of investors, mainly sophisticated investors who have the assets and maturity to comprehend the complicated structure and risks in connection to the securities offerings, then the Securities Act should put such sophisticated investors into a group, namely, the accredited investors.

Section 2(a) of the Securities Act/Reg D-Rule 501(a) defines the term *accredited investors* as follows:

- Individuals with:
    - Net worth of over 1,000,000 USD (excluding residential home)
    - Annual income of more than 200,000 USD (or 300,000 USD as a couple) in the last two years
- Entities with total assets in excess of 5,000,000 USD
- Directors, executive officers, and general partners of the issuer

The most popular way to offer a sale of securities is under Regulation D, Rules 506(b) and 506(c), which are generally considered as the safe harbor under Section 4(a)(2). Offerings made under the rule 506 safe harbor will preempt the state securities requirements, which means that if the offering of securities satisfies the exemption requirements under Rule 506, it will be exempted under the states' securities laws.

Rule 506(b) states the following:

- Under Rule 506(b), the issuer cannot make general solicitations and general advertising. But it allows the issuer to offer the securities to a maximum of 35 non-accredited investors provided that such non-accredited investors are so called *sophisticated investors* or such non-accredited investors making the investment decision as advised by a purchaser representative. In addition, any non-accredited investor must receive a substantive disclosure document that includes financial statements.
- Under Rule 506(b), as long as the issuer has a reasonable belief that the investor is an accredited investor for example if the issuer provides the investor a questionnaire in which the investor shows that they are an accredited investor it will satisfy the requirement under Rule 506(b).

Rule 506(c) states the following:

- The JOBS Act in 2015 also provides a new type of exemption that allows the issuer to use general solicitation and general advertising for its offerings, but with a stricter scrutiny of the qualifications of the investors.
- First, under Rule 506(c), all investors must be accredited creditors. Second, the issuer is required to take reasonable steps to verify that all investors are in fact accredited investors. The SEC provided some nonexclusive methods to verify the status of the accredited investor of individuals, such as asking for W-2 or bank statements of such individual investors.

However, some issuers consider such verification methods as intrusive, so this exemption is not as popular as the Rule 506(b) exemption.

Section 3(b)(1)/ Rule 504 – small issuance

The less popular exemption for a securities offering under Regulation D is Rule 504. Under Rule 504, the issuer can only offer an aggregate total amount of securities up to 5,000,000 USD in a 12-month period. This is considered as a small issuance exemption and is sort of overlapped by Tier 1 under Regulation A+.

Limitation of Rule 504 and 506 – bad actor disqualifications

Both offerings under Rule 504 and Rule 506 under Regulation D are subject to limitation under Rule 506(d), which is known as the **bad actor disqualification**.

As a result of Rule 506(d), bad actor the disqualification, an offering is disqualified from relying on Rules 506(b) and 506(c) of the Regulation D exemption if the issuer or any other person covered by Rule 506(d) has a relevant criminal conviction, regulatory or court order, or other disqualifying event that occurred on or after September 23, 2013, the effective date of the rule amendments. Under Rule 506(e), for disqualifying events that occurred before September 23, 2013, issuers may still rely on Rule 506, but will have to comply with the disclosure provisions of Rule 506(e).

A disqualifying event is usually one of the following:

- Certain criminal convictions
- Certain court injunctions and restraining orders
- Final orders of certain state and federal regulators
- Certain SEC disciplinary orders
- Certain SEC cease-and-desist orders
- SEC stop orders and orders suspending the Regulation A exemption
- Suspension or expulsion from the membership of a self-regulatory organization, for example, the **Financial Industry Regulatory Authority (FINRA)**
- US Postal Service false representation orders

However, actions taken outside of the US will not trigger the disqualification under Rule 506(d).

The bad actors are defined as the following:

- Issuer, predecessor of issuer, or any affiliated issuer
- Any director, executive officer, other officer participating in the offering, general partner, or managing member of the issuer
- Beneficial owner of 20% or more of the issuer's outstanding voting equity securities
- Any promoter connected to the issuer in any capacity at the time of the sale of securities
- Any investment manager of an issuer that is a pooled investment fund

- Any person who has been or will be paid remuneration directly or indirectly for the solicitation of purchasers in connection with the sale of securities
- Any general partner or managing member of any such investment manager or solicitor
- Any director, executive officer, or other officer participating in the offering of any such investment manager or solicitor or general partner or managing member of such investment manager or solicitor

 Some of the disqualifying events may provide a **look-back period**. A look-back period is measured from the date of the disqualifying event (such as the date of the issuance of the court order) instead of the date of the underlying conduct that led to the disqualifying event.

Section 4(a)(5) – accredited investor exemption

Section 4(a)(5) is a very limited exemption, as it only allows the offerings of securities with a total amount of more than USD 5,000,000 to one or more accredited investor(s) without using general solicitation and public advertising; however, this exemption is not limited by the bad actor disqualification. Hence, for offerings that involve a bad actor disqualification, this is a useful tool.

Section 4(a)(6) / Regulation Crowdfunding – crowdfunding exemption

The JOBS Act of 2012 added Section 4(a)(6) to the Securities Act, which provides an exemption from registration for certain crowdfunding transactions. In 2015, the SEC adopted Regulation Crowdfunding to implement the requirements under the JOBS Act. Under the rules, eligible companies will be allowed to raise capital using Regulation Crowdfunding, starting May 16, 2016.

Offerings under Section 4(a)(6) and Regulation Crowdfunding preempts the state law requirements. The aggregated total amount of securities offerings under crowdfunding by each issuer and its affiliates (note: not each offering) cannot exceed 1,070,000 USD with the following additional requirements:

- The crowdfunding cannot be offered by a non-US issuer, reporting company, investment company, and private fund.

- Individuals investment limits:
    - Individuals with either an annual income or a net worth of less than 107,00 USD can only invest the greater of 2,200 USD and 5% of the lesser of investors' net worth or annual income.
    - Individuals with both an annual income and a net worth greater than 107,000 USD may invest 10% of the lesser of the investors' annual income and net worth (not to exceed 107,000 USD per individual investor).
- The issuer needs to file Form C with the SEC prior to offering and after completion of offering the Form C file with the SEC annually.
- Registration of Funding Portal—the issuer who collects crowdfunding must register with the SEC as an intermediary (other than the broker).

As is the case with the exemptions under Regulation D, exemption under Regulation Crowdfunding is also subject to bad actor disqualification.

Section 3(a)(11) / Rule 147 (added by JOBS Act 2012) – intrastate offering

Under Section 3(a)(11) and Rule 147, there is a very limited exemption if the issuer offers and sells its securities only in one specific state.

Regulatory issues with respect to exemptions under the Securities Act

For all the securities offerings conducted under exemptions under the Securities Act, there are several legal issues the issuers need to be reminded of:

- **Notice filing requirements**: First, though the offerings of securities are exempt under Section 5 of the Securities Act, the issuers still must file a notice. For an offerings exemption under Section 4(a)(2), Regulation D and (that is, Rule 504 506) Section 4(a)(5), the issuers need to file Form D which contains the basic information of the securities offerings with the SEC within 15 days after the first sale, which is the date on which the first investor becomes irrevocably contractually committed to invest. Depending on the terms of the contract between the issuer and the investor, this could be the date on which the issuer receives the investor's signed subscription agreement or payment for the securities.

- For crowdfunding offerings, the issuers need to file Form C, which should include the information in a brief business overview containing the target-offering amount, selected offering details, intermediary information, and financial and other information about the issuer. The issuer needs to file Form C online through the SEC's filing website.

- **Transaction-specific exemptions**: Second, the issuer should note that each of the preceding exemptions covers only a specific transaction that is, the offerings made at a specific time. If subsequent offerings of the same type of securities are made, such offerings have to satisfy the requirements under any of the exemptions.

- **Integration doctrine**: Third, even if the offerings satisfy each of the exemptions at each time that the offerings are made, there is an integration rule that the SEC will consider any offerings made within a six-month period as one big transaction, and this means that each transaction may taint the other transaction(s) and hence disqualify the other transactions under the relevant exemptions.

- **Securities offered under exemptions are restricted securities**: Fourth, the securities offered under an exemption under the section of the Securities Act are considered restricted securities, which should not be available for sale or be tradable in a public secondary market. Resale of restricted securities must satisfy separate exemption requirements.

- Fifth, the issuers must know that even though the initial offerings of securities are exempted under the registration requirements, a subsequent sale of such securities must separately satisfy the exemption under the Securities Act.

Other related regulatory regimes

In this section, we will cover primary regulatory regimes, as well as other related regulatory regimes as shown in the following list:

- **Security fraud Rule 10b-5**: The offering materials for STC/ICO may be subject to Rule 10b-5, which is an important rule targeting securities fraud promulgated by the US SEC, pursuant to its authority granted under § 10(b) of the Securities Exchange Act of 1934. The rule prohibits any act or omission resulting in fraud or deceit in connection with the purchase or sale of any security.

- **Securities trading platform – Securities Exchange Act of 1934**: The entity that trades and provides trading platforms of securities tokens may also be subject to the Securities Exchange Act of 1934.

  Section 15(a) of the Exchange Act states that, without qualifying for an exception or exemption, it is unlawful for any broker or dealer to make use of the mails or any means or instrumentality of interstate commerce to effect any transactions in, or to induce or attempt to induce the purchase or sale, of any security if such broker or dealer is not registered in accordance with Section 15(b) of the Exchange Act.

  Section 3(a)(4) of the Exchange Act generally defines a *broker* as any person, including a company, engaged in the business of effecting transactions in securities for the account of others.

  Section 3(a)(5) of the Exchange Act generally defines a *dealer* as any person, including a company, engaged in the business of buying and selling securities for that person's own account through a broker or otherwise.

- **Issuers – Investment Company Act of 1940**: If an investment entity, such as a fund or issuer of tokens, is considered *a* pooled investment vehicle formed by the founder for the purpose of investing in certain digital tokens issued by others, it may be subject to registration as an investment company under the Investment Company Act of 1940, unless the applicable exemptions apply to it.

  A fund investing in security tokens may fall under the definitions of an investment company if either of the following applies:

  - Under the operation test, the issuer is or holds itself out as being engaged primarily or proposes to engage primarily in the business of investing in securities
  - Under the balance sheet test, the issuer is engaged or proposes to engage in the business of investing, reinvesting, owning, holding, or trading in securities, and holds or proposes to hold more than 40% of its assets in securities

  There are two types of exemptions, the so-called private investment company exemptions that are applicable to such investment funds in crypto tokens:

  - Section 3(c)(1) exempts those issuers with fewer than 100 individual beneficial owners and does not make any public offering of their securities.

- Section 3(c)(7) exempts those issuers whose outstanding securities are owned exclusively by qualified purchasers who are basically investors with more than USD 5 million (for individuals, trusts, and closely held family offices) and USD 25 million (for companies and investment managers). But there is no limit to the number of investors of the issuer.

An investment company that neither registers nor falls under any applicable exemption will basically render any contracts previously entered unenforceable.

- **Investment Advisers Act of 1940**: Under the Investment Advisers Act of 1940, an investment adviser is defined as any person or group that makes investment recommendations or conducts securities analysis in return for a fee, whether through the direct management of client assets or via written publications. An investment adviser who has sufficient assets to be registered with the SEC is known as a **registered investment adviser**.

Federal regulators

As federal agencies, regulators are responsible for regulating and overseeing the financial system in the following ways:

- The SEC protects investors, maintains fair, orderly, and efficient markets, and facilitates capital formation by promulgating securities regulations, enforcing these regulatory rules. The SEC oversees the key participants in the securities market, including securities exchanges, securities brokers and dealers, investment advisers, and mutual funds. The SEC is concerned primarily with promoting the disclosure of important market-related information, maintaining fair dealing, and protecting against fraud.
- The **Financial Crimes Enforcement Network** (**FinCEN**) safeguards the financial system from illicit use, combats money laundering, and promotes national security through the strategic use of financial authorities and the collection, analysis, and dissemination of financial intelligence. FinCEN supplements the SEC's works.

- The **Department of Justice** (**DOJ**) starts investigations into US securities violations and prosecute violators under criminal charges.

State regulations

The following cryptocurrency regulations were issued in US states:

- The **New York State Department of Financial Services** (**NYSDFS**) issued the requirements to acquire a BitLicense in order to trade virtual currencies, including bitcoin, in the state of New York.
- The **Uniform Regulation of Virtual Currency Business Act** (**URVCBA**). In July 2017, the Uniform Law Commission completed a uniform model state law, known as the **Uniform Regulation of the Virtual Currency Businesses Act** (**URVCBA** or **the Act**).

Each state has its own securities laws and regulations, as well as its security registration requirements.

Resale of securities Rule 144/144A/Section 4(a)(1½) / Section 4(a)(7)

Securities issued in an unregistered offering under the exemptions mentioned previously are restricted securities. In order to transfer or resell the restricted security by the holder, it has to be either registered or exempt from the registration requirement, which is a separate requirement from its initial offering.

The secondary sale of such restricted securities in the US is governed under these rules.

Rule 144 exemption

The Rule 144 exemption is a safe harbor provision. This allows nonaffiliate public resales of a private company's restricted securities after a one-year holding period by the security holder.

Rule 144A exemption

Rule 144A allows the resale of restricted securities only to **qualified institutional buyers** (**QIBs**) who are institutions that own or invest on a discretionary basis at least US $100 million of securities and are considered the most sophisticated investors.

Section 4(a)(1½) exemption

The so-called Section 4(a)(1½) resale is not formally established by any written rule or regulation. It has just been developed over time by securities professionals. It was used as a basis to allow for the resale of restricted securities among sophisticated investors who could buy securities at a private resale of restricted securities without much protection of the Securities Act registration and offering materials delivery requirements.

Section 4(a)(7) exemption

This is a new resale exemption added in 2015. It requires that the resales can only be made to each purchaser who is an accredited investor without using general solicitation or general advertising and with certain information requirements for nonreporting issuers.

Securities laws development in blockchain and digital cryptocurrencies

After an overview of the US securities laws and regulations, we now turn to how the SEC gradually became involved in regulating digital tokens offerings and trading. We will review the SEC's analysis of how the current securities regulations apply to this regime as new issues emerge.

Some of the early warnings and guideline on investments in digital tokens are as follows.

SEC alerts

Let's look at the following few alerts:

- **Alert on the use of Bitcoin as a Ponzi scheme in July 2013 – SEC versus Shavers**:

  This early alert made by the SEC involving digital tokens was based on the Shavers case in 2013.

  In that case, the organizer of an alleged Ponzi scheme advertised a Bitcoin investment opportunity in an online Bitcoin forum, where the organizer promised investors up to 7% interest every week. The organizer stated that it would use the invested funds for Bitcoin arbitrage activities and make profits for the investors. However, instead of investing in bitcoins, the organizer used the funds to pay existing investors and pay the organizer's personal expenses.

  With respect to the scheme based on new technology, the SEC alert states the following:

  > *"Fraudsters are not beyond the reach of the SEC just because they use Bitcoin or another virtual currency to mislead investors and violate the federal securities laws. Shavers preyed on investors in an online forum by claiming his investments carried no risk and huge profits for them while his true intentions were rooted in nothing more than personal greed."*
  >
  > *– Andrew M Calamari, Director of the SEC's New York Regional Office*

  The SEC's investor alert reminds investors to be wary of investment opportunities that promise high rates of return with little or no risk, especially when dealing with unregistered, internet-based investments sold by unlicensed organizers.

- **Alert on Bitcoin and other virtual-currency-related investments in May, 2014**:

  Another early alert issued by SEC involved Bitcoin and virtual currency in 2014. In this instance, the SEC warned that as Bitcoin's price fluctuated dramatically on the market, some Bitcoin investors may have increased their wealth quickly at some point but then decreased their wealth as the market went into downturn soon after.

The SEC alert states the following:

> *"The rise of Bitcoin and other virtual and digital currencies creates new concerns for investors. A new product, technology, or innovation – such as Bitcoin – has the potential to give rise both to frauds and high-risk investment opportunities. Potential investors can be easily enticed with the promise of high returns in a new investment space and also may be less skeptical when assessing something novel, new and cutting-edge.*
>
> *Both fraudsters and promoters of high-risk investment schemes may target Bitcoin users. The exchange rate of U.S. dollars to bitcoins has fluctuated dramatically since the first bitcoins were created. As the exchange rate of Bitcoin is significantly higher today, many early adopters of Bitcoin may have experienced an unexpected increase in wealth, making them attractive targets for fraudsters as well as promoters of high-risk investment opportunities.*
>
> *Fraudsters target any group they think they can convince to trust them. Scam artists may take advantage of Bitcoin users' vested interest in the success of Bitcoin to lure these users into Bitcoin related investment schemes. The fraudsters may be (or pretend to be) Bitcoin users themselves. Similarly, promoters may find Bitcoin users to be a receptive audience for legitimate but high-risk investment opportunities. Fraudsters and promoters may solicit investors through forums and online sites frequented by members of the Bitcoin community."*

- **FINRA Alert 2015 – risk of buying and using digital currency such as Bitcoin**:

In this alert, the FINRA states the following:

> *"Investors should know that buying and using digital currency such as Bitcoin carry risks. Speculative trading in bitcoins carries significant risk. There is also the risk of fraud related to companies claiming to offer Bitcoin payment platforms and other Bitcoin-related products and services."*
>
> *"When the SEC first brought the Texas case involving bitcoins, it issued a warning about the potential for fraud. As with so many other hot or new trends, fraudsters may see the latest digital currency trend as a chance to steal your money through old-fashioned fraud."*

However, all these warnings, alerts, and guidelines did not define whether the digital tokens offered are securities. As there are more and more digital token offerings in recent years, this raised the concerns of the SEC. Finally, in 2017, SEC issued a report of investigation, the so-called **Decentralized Autonomous Organization (DAO)** report that provided an analysis on whether a digital token could be considered as a security.

Report of Investigation Pursuant to Section 21(a) of the Exchange Act – The DAO (July 25, 2017) (the DAO report) – the application of the Howey test

In the DAO report, the SEC studied the case of the DAO as an example of fundraising by a virtual organization embodied in computer code and executed on a distributed ledger or blockchain. The SEC provided an analysis on whether the DAO had violated US federal securities laws. This is the most thorough and complete analysis from the SEC on security tokens offerings to date and provides general guidance for a token issuer who uses a DAO entity or other distributed ledger or blockchain-enabled means for fundraising.

The key facts of the case are as follows:

- The DAO was an incorporated virtual organization created by Slock.it, a German company, and its founders in 2016 to attract investments through the sale of tokens (DAO tokens) to investors, and such investments would be used to fund projects in order to make profits.
- The investors of DAO tokens would later share the profits derived from these projects as a return on their investments in DAO tokens.
- Moreover, the DAO token holders could monetize their investments in DAO tokens by reselling based on the issuer's promise that DAO tokens would be traded on a number of web-based platforms that supported secondary trading in the DAO tokens.
- During the offering period, the DAO sold around 1.15 billion DAO tokens (in exchange for a total of about 12 million ether (ETH)), which was valued at approximately USD 150 million.
- The founder of Slock.it described the DAO as for profit and an effort to create a crowdfunding contract to raise funds to grow a company in the crypto space.

- The white paper of the DAO described the investment opportunity as the first implementation of a code to automate organizational governance and decision making, and said that it could be used by individuals working together outside the traditional corporate form. The system should be autonomous where the project proposals (in the form of smart contracts) were posted on the Ethereum blockchain, and the votes were carried out by the code of the DAO.

- However, the setup of the voting process would give some control by the founders of Slock.it, who chose the curators to review, select, and determine which proposals would be subject to voting by all DAO token holders. The curators had the ultimate discretion as to whether to submit a proposal for voting, and determined that on the order and frequency of proposals should be whitelisted for voting. The mechanism of voting was arranged in a way that token holders had to pledge a certain token in order to vote. The tokens pledged were not allowed to be transferred or traded until the end of the voting cycle. This meant that either token holders had to vote *yes* or not to vote at all in order to have free transferability of their tokens.

- After launch, the DAO tokens were traded on electronic platforms using virtual or fiat currencies. From May 2016 to September 2016, there were about 580,000 buy and sell transactions of the DAO token by more than 15,700 of US and foreign customers of the electronic platforms on the secondary markets. This is a large secondary market.

Legal analysis by the SEC

As mentioned earlier, under Section 5 of the Securities Act of 1933, as amended, the offer or sale of securities in the US to the public must be registered unless it falls under the exemptions.

The SEC first explains that the foundational principles of the securities apply to virtual organizations or capital-raising entities making use of distributed ledger technology. Therefore, the US securities law will apply to an ICO if it is targeted to the public in the US.

The issue is whether the offer or sale of a digital token will be considered an offer or sale of a "security" under US securities law. The closest term to be applied to the issuance of DAO tokens is whether the DAO token will be considered as an investment contract. The DAO report provided a thorough analysis by using the traditional **Howey test**.

Under the Howey test, an **investment contract** is "*an investment of money in a common enterprise with a reasonable expectation of profits to be derived from the entrepreneurial or managerial efforts of others.*"

In analyzing whether something is a security, form should be disregarded for substance, and the emphasis should be on economic realities underlying a transaction.

Basically, this seems to mean that it does not matter what you called it. If the so-called utility tokens being offered or sold have a security nature and satisfy the Howey test, they will be considered securities and will be covered under the securities law and the regime of the SEC.

The process to identify a security involves the following information:

- **Investment of money**: In the DAO case, the issuer offered and sold DAO tokens to investors in exchange for their ETH as their investments. This activity was regarded a contribution of value that can be considered as an investment contract under the Howey test.
- **Common enterprise**: The DAO token investors' ETH, the investments, were put in the DAO—that is, the common enterprise. With their investments in DAO, the investors reasonably expected to earn profits through this common enterprise when they put their ETH into the DAO's Ethereum blockchain address in exchange for DAO tokens.
- **Reasonable expectation of profits**: The promotional materials regarding DAO investments described it as a for-profit entity for the purposes of generating profits though funding projects with profitable prospects. When they made their investments, DAO token holders were convinced by the promotional materials and expected that they would derive and share in future profits from the projects funded by the DAO.
- **Entrepreneurial or managerial efforts of others**: The way the DAO operated was that Slock.it and its cofounders put in a lot of effort in actively maintaining and overseeing the DAO's operations. The DAO curators appointed by the Slock.it founders had the power to determine whether a proposal should be put to a vote by DAO token investors. Slock.it and its cofounders monitored the DAO closely and addressed issues as they arose. As a result, investors' profits would be derived from the managerial efforts of Slock.it, its cofounders, and the DAO curators.

Although DAO token investors might have been able to vote on which projects they should fund, these voting rights were limited because the curators were the ones with the control over which proposals should be whitelisted for a vote by DAO token investors. Therefore, the DAO token investors could only vote on the proposals selected by the curators.

In fact, DAO token investors had to and did rely on the significant managerial efforts provided by Slock.it and its cofounders and the DAO's curators to operate the DAO and make profits.

SEC's conclusion

The SEC concluded that the issuance of DAO tokens is considered an offering of security and hence this would be covered under the Securities Act. Therefore, the issuer must register such an offer regarding the sale of such DAO tokens. Issuers also include any unincorporated organization such as the DAO.

The SEC also concluded that the DAO is required to register the offer and sale of DAO tokens, unless a valid exemption from such a registration applied. Otherwise, those who participated in an unregistered offer and sale of securities not subject to a valid exemption are liable for violating Section 5 of the Securities Act.

Security trading

In addition, the SEC also concluded that as the DAO tokens were traded on electronic platforms using virtual or fiat currencies, such trading of DAO tokens will be considered as the trading of security. Hence, those trading platforms that provided a secondary market for the buying and selling of DAO tokens should be required to register with the SEC under Section 5 of the Securities Exchange Act of 1934, as there is no applicable exemption in this case.

The DAO reports provide a quick and clear analysis on how the SEC approached such a type of digital tokens offering, and it is a reliable guideline for token issuers to follow; however, as the SEC summarized at the end of the analysis, *whether or not a particular transaction involves the offer and sale of a security, regardless of the terminology used, will depend on the facts and circumstances, including the economic realities of the transaction.* As a result, an issuer, before launching an STO, should carefully consider the nature of the tokens being offered, the mechanism of the investment in these tokens, the use of these tokens, the control of the DAO, how the investors will be rewarded, and the expectations of the token holders. Each case has its unique circumstances and considerations, so it is recommended that a thorough legal analysis is conducted before launching the issuance of the tokens.

Real cases

The following real cases will show how the organizations in question violated federal securities laws under the SEC's reviews and the failure to file registration for the offering of digital tokens with the SEC.

Munchee Inc. (Munchee order, December 11, 2017)

In the Munchee case, the SEC applied the analysis from the DAO report.

The facts of the case are as follows:

- Munchee has its place of business in California. It created an iPhone application (the Munchee app) in the US for the public to post pictures, review meals, and rate restaurants. Munchee's staff maintained and upgraded the Munchee app.
- Munchee and its agents had control of the content on multiple web pages, which included a Twitter account, a Facebook page, and its own website (the Munchee website).
- It posted a white paper (the *MUN White Paper*) through Facebook, Twitter, Bitcointalk, and the Munchee website, where it provided descriptions of MUN tokens, the offering process, how proceeds received from the offering of MUN would be used to develop its business (so as to improve its existing app and recruit users to buy advertisements, write reviews, sell food, and conduct other transactions using MUN. The *MUN White Paper* stated that "*as currently designed, the sale of MUN utility tokens does not pose a significant risk of implicating federal securities laws*", making reference to the DAO report and a Howey analysis. However, such analysis cannot be found in the *MUN White Paper*.
- During the offering period, Munchee offered and sold digital tokens (MUN or MUN tokens) through a blockchain or a distributed ledger and planned to raise about $15 million in capital.
- Later, the SEC challenged the ICO of the MUN token because the offering was not registered, nor did it fall into any exemptions of securities registration. Munchee then offered a settlement for this case with the SEC.

Legal analysis by the SEC

The Munchee case refers to the Howey test applied to the DAO report, in which the SEC stated that tokens, coins, or other digital assets issued on a blockchain may be considered securities under the federal securities laws under the Howey test. Hence, issuers who offer or sell digital tokens that will be identified as securities in the US should register the offering and sale with the SEC unless it qualifies for an exemption from registration.

As in the DAO report, the SEC used the Howey test to determine whether a digital token should be classed as a security—that is, whether it satisfies the following four requirements of an investment contract:

- **Investment of money**: Munchee offered and sold MUN tokens to potential investors in the US through a method of general solicitation. Similar to the case in DAO, the investors invested Ether or Bitcoin in exchange for their MUN tokens. This investment can be considered as a type of contribution of value, creating an investment contract.

- **Common enterprise**: From the information provided by Munchee, investors, while making their investments in MUN tokens, had a reasonable expectation of profits from their investment in Munchee, the common enterprise. Munchee stated that proceeds of the MUN token offering would be used by Munchee to build an ecosystem that would create demand for MUN tokens and make MUN tokens more valuable. Munchee also stated that it would revise the Munchee app so that more people could buy and sell services with MUN tokens. It also stated that it would recruit partners such as restaurants that would accept MUN tokens as payment for meals. As a result, the investors reasonably expected that they would derive profit from the increase in the value of MUN tokens created by the revised Munchee app and by Munchee's ability to create an ecosystem, which was described in the offering as a system where, on the one hand, restaurants would want to use MUN tokens to buy advertising from Munchee or to pay rewards to app users, and, on the other hand, app users would want to use MUN tokens to pay for restaurant meals and would want to write reviews to obtain MUN tokens.

- **Reasonable expectation of profits**: Munchee emphasized to investors that it would be a secondary trading market for MUN tokens after the offering of MUN tokens. Based on Munchee's statements, the investors reasonably expected to profit from the increase in value of MUN tokens resulting from Munchee's efforts in the operation of its business.

- **Entrepreneurial or managerial efforts of others**: Investors in the MUN tokens did not directly involve themselves in Munchee's business. They expected to derive profits from Munchee by the significant entrepreneurial and managerial efforts of others; that is, Munchee's team and agents were expected to maintain and revise the Munchee app and create the ecosystem that would increase the value of the MUN tokens and support secondary markets of the MUN tokens.

When the sale of MUN tokens began with the initial offering, these tokens appeared to have a practical use. However, the SEC said that this wouldn't prevent the token from being a security. Determining whether a security is involved in a transaction doesn't turn on the labeling of the tokens—for example, if an ICO was characterized as one with a utility token. Instead, it required the customers to consider the underlying economic realities in a transaction. All pertinent conditions and facts should be taken into account while making that determination.

The SEC concluded that Munchee offered and sold securities to the general public, including potential investors in the US, without filing any registration statements with the SEC, nor did it fall under any available exemptions from registration. As a result, Munchee violated the Securities Act, which states that unless a registration statement is filed with the SEC with respect to a security, it shall be unlawful for any person, directly or indirectly, to sell any security without any available exemption.

AirFox case (November, 2018)

The facts of the **AirFox** case are as follows:

- AirFox was formed in Massachusetts. It sold mobile technology that allowed customers of certain prepaid mobile telecommunications operators in the US to earn free or discounted airtime or data by interacting with advertisements on their smartphones. AirFox decided to launch a new consumer business line in 2017 by providing an internet browser application (the AirFox app) that could be downloaded from the Google Play Store, and told people that users of Android-based smartphones could earn AirTokens by viewing advertisements in the AirFox app. AirFox mentioned that the AirTokens could be exchanged for free airtime or data from multiple prepaid mobile telecommunications providers.
- Later, AirFox published a business plan stating that it would raise capital through the sale of AirTokens and introduced an AirFox Apple application that would allow users to earn AirTokens, which could be exchanged for free or discounted mobile data and other goods and services.
- In connection with the offering, AirFox stated that AirTokens would increase in value as a result of AirFox's efforts, and that AirFox would undertake efforts to provide investors with liquidity by making AirTokens tradable on secondary markets. The AirFox's whitepaper also stated that when investors paid ether or other forms of valuable e-currency for AirTokens, they were contributing to the development of the AirToken Project—that is, the creation of an AirTokens ecosystem.

- AirTokens were tokens issued on the Ethereum blockchain. AirFox advertised its forthcoming offering of AirTokens by posting a white paper on its website and providing additional information via blog posts, social media posts, online videos, and discussion boards. AirFox's advertisements described AirTokens, the offering process, how AirFox would use the offering proceeds to develop its business, the way in which AirTokens would increase in value, and the ability for AirToken holders to trade AirTokens on secondary markets.
- AirFox wanted its investors to agree that they were buying AirTokens for their utility as a means of exchange for mobile airtime, and not as an investment or a security; however, at the time of the ICO, this functionality was not available and the AirFox app was just a prototype that only enabled users to earn and redeem loyalty points that could be exchanged for mobile airtime.
- From August to October, 2017, AirFox offered and sold its digital tokens (AirTokens issued on a blockchain or distributed ledger). Through this ICO, AirFox raised approximately $15 million in capital. At the time of the ICO, AirFox indicated to investors that the proceeds of the offering would be used to fund future development of the AirFox app and the AirToken ecosystem.

Legal analysis by the SEC

Referring to the Howey test applied to the DAO report, the SEC stated that tokens, coins, or other digital assets issued on a blockchain may be classed as securities under the federal securities laws under the Howey test. Hence, issuers who offer or sell digital tokens that are identified as securities in the US shall register the offering and sale of them with the SEC unless the issuer qualifies for an exemption from registration.

As in the DAO report, the SEC used the Howey test to determine whether a digital token should be a security—that is, whether it satisfied the four requirements of an investment contract:

- **Investment of money**: AirFox offered and sold AirTokens to potential investors in the United States through general solicitation. Similar to the DAO and Munchee case, the investors invested in ETH in exchange for their AirTokens. This investment can be considered as a type of contribution of value, creating an investment contract.
- **Common enterprise**: The investors of AirToken invested ETH in exchange for AirTokens. AirFox stated that proceeds of the AirToken offering would be used by AirFox, the common enterprise, to build an ecosystem that would create demand for AirTokens, which would increase the value of AirTokens.

- **Reasonable expectation of profits**: The investors, according to information provided by AirFox, expected that the company would improve the AirFox app, add new functionality, enter into agreements with third-party telecommunication companies, and take other steps to encourage the use of AirTokens and foster the growth of the ecosystem. Investors reasonably expected they would profit from the success of AirFox's efforts to grow the ecosystem and the rise in the value of AirTokens.
- **Entrepreneurial or managerial efforts of others**: Investors of AirTokens did not directly involve themselves in AirFox's business. They expected to derive profits from the significant entrepreneurial and managerial efforts of AirFox and its agents to create the ecosystem that would increase the value of AirTokens and facilitate secondary market trading.

AirTokens, it seemed, would have a practical use after the offering; however, the SEC stated that it would not preclude the token from being a security. The SEC concluded that AirFox offered and sold securities to the general public, including potential investors in the US, without filing any registration statements with the SEC, and that the offering of AirTokens did not fall under any exemptions from registration.

As a result, AirFox violated the Securities Act, which states that unless a registration statement is filed with the SEC with respect to a security, it shall be unlawful for any person, directly or indirectly, to sell any security absent of any available exemption.

The Paragon case (November, 2018)

The facts of the Paragon case were as follows:

- Paragon was an online entity of the cannabis industry that used blockchain technology. In 2017, Paragon released a white paper on its website and social media websites describing its planned business model and upcoming token sale. Paragon's white paper stated that its mission was to *"pull the cannabis community from marginalized to mainstream by building blockchain into every step of the cannabis industry and by working toward full legalization."* Its white paper also listed out the terms of an upcoming token sale that would raise funds to build the various Paragon business segments.

- Paragon and its agents controlled the content of multiple web pages, such as its website, a Twitter account, a Facebook page, and posts on various blogs and message boards (the Paragon web pages). For a period of two months, Paragon offered and sold digital tokens (PRG or PRG tokens) issued on a blockchain, or a distributed ledger (the offering) through crowdfunding, where PRG tokens could be purchased only in exchange for other digital assets, including Bitcoin, Ether, Litecoin, Dashcoin, Zcash, Ripple, Monero, Ethereum Classic, and Waves. PRG tokens could not be purchased with fiat currency.

- Paragon's purpose of offering PRG tokens was to raise capital in developing and implementing its business plan to provide blockchain technology to the cannabis industry and work toward the legalization of cannabis, which also included the purchase of real estate for its ParagonSpaces business segment. In offered materials, Paragon described the way PRG tokens would increase in value based on Paragon's efforts and made statements on internet forums, blogs, emails, and social media stating that the PRG token offering was an opportunity to make money.

- Paragon indicated that PRG tokens would be traded on secondary markets and it would seek to list PRG tokens on various secondary trading platforms. After the offering, PRG tokens were traded on multiple digital asset-trading platforms.

- Paragon raised approximately $12 million worth of digital assets during the offering. Paragon did not register the offering pursuant to the federal securities laws, nor did it attempt to qualify for an exemption to the registration requirements.

Legal analysis by the SEC

Referring to the Howey test applied to the DAO report, the SEC stated that tokens, coins, or other digital assets issued on a blockchain may be considered securities under the federal securities laws as defined by the Howey test. Hence, issuers who offer or sell digital tokens that will be identified as securities in the US should register the offering and sale with the SEC unless it qualifies for an exemption from registration.

As in the DAO report, the SEC used the Howey test to determine whether a digital token should be considered a security—that is, whether it satisfies the following four requirements of an investment contract:

- **Investment of money**: The SEC concluded that potential investors were approached by Paragon through general solicitation in which Paragon offered and sold PRG tokens to them in the US. Similar to the DAO, Munchee, and AirFox cases, the investors invested other digital assets, including bitcoin, ether, Litecoin, Dashcoin, Zcash, Ripple, Monero, Ethereum Classic, and Waves, and so on, in exchange for their PRG tokens. This investment could be considered as a type of contribution of value, creating an investment contract.

- **Common enterprise**: PRG token investors invested ETH and other digital assets in exchange for PRG tokens. Paragon stated that the proceeds of the PRG token offering would be used by Paragon, the common enterprise, to raise capital in developing and implementing its business plan to provide blockchain technology to the cannabis industry and work toward the legalization of cannabis, which also included the purchase of real estate for its ParagonSpaces business segment. This would increase the value of PRG tokens.

- **Reasonable expectation of profits**: Paragon's marketing scheme of the PRG tokens offer included information on the Paragon web pages, the white paper and message boards, blogs, social media, and other outlets. Such information described how Paragon would build an ecosystem that created demand and increased the value of the PRG tokens. Because of what was said in the marketing materials and conduct of Paragon and its agents, it was reasonable for PRG token investors to believe that they will derive profits from their investments.

- **Entrepreneurial or managerial efforts of others**: PRG token investors reasonably expected to derive profits from the significant entrepreneurial and managerial efforts of others—that is, Paragon and its agents—to create the ecosystem that would increase the value of PRG and support secondary markets. Paragon's marketing information of the PRG token offering caused PRG token investors' to expect a return on their investments, that Paragon and its agents could be relied on to provide the significant entrepreneurial and managerial efforts required to make PRG tokens a success, and that profits would be derived from the operation of Paragon's business in the cannabis industry.

As a result, the SEC concluded that Paragon offered and sold securities to the general public, including investors in the US. Since Paragon did not file any registration statement with respect to the PRG token offers and sales, and such an offering did not qualify for any exemption from registration, Paragon violated Section 5 of the Securities Act.

The following case shows the fraudulent information in offering materials that are a violation of Rule 10b-5.

SEC versus PlexCorps et al.

SEC versus PlexCorps et al., Civil Action No. 17-cv-07007 (E.D. N.Y., filed December 1, 2017) (PlexCorps Litigation)

In this case, the SEC filed for an emergency asset freeze to halt a fast-moving ICO fraud that had raised up to $15 million from thousands of investors since August 2017 by falsely promising a 13-fold profit in less than a month. The SEC filed charges against a recidivist Quebec securities law violator, Dominic Lacroix, and his company, PlexCorps (the defendants). The SEC filed its complaint in federal court in Brooklyn, New York. The SEC also alleged that the defendants had misappropriated investor funds for personal use. The SEC also charged Lacroix's partner, Sabrina Paradis-Royer, in connection with the scheme.

The facts of the case are as follows:

- Lacroix set up PlexCorps in Canada and started to market and sell securities called PlexCoin on Facebook to investors in the US and worldwide. PlexCorps stated that PlexCoin would be considered as the next decentralized worldwide cryptocurrency based on the Ethereum structure and its mission was to broaden the possibilities of its uses and to increase the number of users by simplifying the process of managing cryptocurrency to the maximum.
- Later, Lacroix launched websites for PlexCorps and PlexCoin. On these websites, Lacroix mentioned that investments in PlexCoin would yield a 1,354 % profit on investors' investments in fewer than 30 days.

The following was the SEC's charge:

After becoming aware of the online content and the conduct of the defendants, the SEC filed a complaint at the federal court, charging Lacroix, Paradis-Royer, and PlexCorps with violating the anti-fraud provisions and misappropriating funds, and Lacroix and PlexCorps with violating the registration requirements of the US federal securities laws. The SEC specifically sought an officer-and-director bar against Lacroix and a bar from offering digital securities against Lacroix and Paradis-Royer.

This was the court's decision:

Without having the defendants appearing at the court, the New York district federal court decided that the SEC had made a substantial showing of the likelihood of success on the merits of the securities violation under Sections 5 and 17(a) of the Securities Act; Section 10(b) of the Exchange Act; and SEC Rule 10b-5. Moreover, the court considered that the SEC likely would establish that PlexCorps participated in a fraud to illegally obtain more than $15 million in proceeds by offering PlexCoin tokens, which are considered as investment contracts subject to the Securities Act and Exchange Act.

The court also considered that the defendants were likely to repeat these illegal activities that the SEC tried to prove; based on the risk of repetition, the court decided to freeze PlexCorps's assets in order to preserve the status quo and to protect the court's ability to award relief to the investors who had suffered from this fraud. As a result, the court granted the SEC's motion.

The following case shows how issuers failed to register as an investment company with SEC.

Crypto Asset Management case (September, 2018)

The facts of the case are as follows.

The founder of the fund formed three entities in the fund structure:

- Crypto Asset Management, LP, the manager, which is a Delaware limited partnership operating in California
- Crypto Asset Management GP, LLC, which serve as the general partner.
- Crypto Asset Fund, LLC, the fund, was a pooled investment vehicle formed for the purpose of investing in digital assets. It was a Delaware limited liability company with its principal place of business in La Jolla, California that focused on investing in digital assets. This was the founder's first US-based fund.

During the fundraising period between August 1, 2017 and December 1, 2017, the fund had raised more than $3.6 million from 44 investors, who were primarily individuals residing in at least 15 states in the US. The fund and the manager did not have any pre-existing relationships with these investors and they approached these investors by general solicitation through its website, social media accounts, and traditional media outlet interviews. Neither the founder nor the manager filed any registration statement with the SEC and no exemption from registration was available during the fundraising period.

The founder and manager controlled and directed the investment of the fund's assets. The manager earned incentive and management fees from the fund according to the terms of its management agreement with the fund. The founder received distributions from the manager according to the manager's limited partnership agreement.

After fundraising, the fund was involved in the business of investing, holding, and trading certain digital assets that were considered investments in securities. Such investments in securities constituted a value exceeding 40% of the value of the fund's total, which caused the fund to fall under the definition of an *investment company*, yet the fund did not register with the SEC as an investment company, nor did it meet any statutory exemptions or fall under exclusions from the definition of an investment company.

The manager, in the company's marketing materials, also negligently misrepresented to investors that the fund was the first regulated crypto asset fund in the US and that it had filed a registration statement with the SEC. The manager did not take any reasonable steps to ensure the accuracy of such statements before publicizing them to the investors.

Legal analysis by the SEC

Based on the preceding conduct, the SEC charged the funder, the manager, and the fund with four violations:

- First, the SEC concluded that the fundraising activities constituted an offering of securities; however, as they did not file any registration statement with the SEC, nor did the offering fall under any appropriate exemption from registration, they willfully violated Section 5(a) of the Securities Act, which prohibits the sale of securities through interstate commerce.
- Second, the fund was involved in the business of investing, holding, and trading certain digital assets that were considered investment securities, and since such investments in the securities constituted a value exceeding 40% of the value of the fund's total, that caused the fund to fall under the definition of investment company. However, the fund did not register with the SEC as an investment company, nor did it meet any statutory exemptions or exclusions from the definition of an investment company. As a result, the manager caused the fund's violation of Section 7(a) of the Investment Company Act, which states that an investment company not registered with the SEC is prohibited from engaging in any business in offering, selling, purchasing, or redeeming interests in the investment company.

- Third, regarding the company's marketing materials, the manager negligently misrepresented to investors that the fund was the first regulated crypto asset fund in the US and that it had filed a registration statement with the SEC, which were untrue statements because the fund did not file any registration with SEC and the offering during fundraising was not exempted under the registration requirement. Hence, the manager violated Section 17(a)(2) of the Securities Act, which prohibits any person involved in the offer or sale of securities from obtaining money or property by means of any untrue statement of material fact or any omission to state a material fact necessary in order to make the statements made not misleading.
- Fourth, the manager provided investment advice to the founder and general partner of the fund as an investment adviser, and the manager made the preceding untrue statements regarding the registration of the fund, so the manager violated Section 206(4) of the Advisers Act and Rule 206(4)-8, which make it unlawful for any investment adviser to a pooled investment vehicle that is, the fund—to make any untrue statement of a material fact or to omit to state a material fact necessary to make the statements made, in the light of the circumstances under which they were made, not misleading, to any investor or prospective investor in the pooled investment vehicle.

The following case shows a case where the trading platforms of digital tokens failed to register as exchanges with the SEC.

The TokenLot LLC case (September, 2018)

The facts of the case are as follows:

- TokenLot was formed in Michigan as a limited liability company. It marketed and sold digital tokens to investors through an online platform. There were two owners operating the platform. It has never been registered with the SEC in any capacity.
- TokenLot called itself ICO Superstore and it operated as an unregistered broker-dealer by publicly offering customers the ability to buy, sell, and trade digital assets connected to ICOs from July, 2017 through late February, 2018. It put advertisements on its website and sold digital tokens that were considered as securities to retail investors using its platform.
- Through soliciting potential investors, the owners of TokenLot processed thousands of customer orders for digital tokens, processed investor funds, and processed more than 200 different digital tokens with respect to ICOs conducted by other entities and its secondary market activities on its platform.

- The owners of TokenLot, through the online platform, received more than 5,800 purchase orders from investors and executed 2,100 of them with respect to 9 digital tokens connected to ICOs. Moreover, the owners of TokenLot sold about 145 digital tokens in secondary market trading through the platform, which constituted 1,650 purchase orders from investors. They also promoted the sale of about 40 digital tokens in exchange for marketing fees paid by digital token issuers. The owners received about $471,000 in total in compensation from the previously mentioned activities.

Legal analysis by the SEC

The SEC's conclusion was that digital assets issued and traded by TokenLot *were* securities, and the SEC charged TokenLot and its owners with violating broker-dealer registration requirements under the Exchange Act, and also alleged that they engaged in unregistered offers and sales of securities in violation of Section 5 of the Securities Act. TokenLot and its owner have submitted offers of settlement (*offers*) that the SEC has determined to accept.

Moreover, the SEC concluded that TokenLot and its owners violated Section 15(a) of the Exchange Act, which provides that, without an exception or exemption, it is unlawful for any broker or dealer *to involve in the purchase or sale, of any security unless such broker or dealer is registered in accordance with Section 15(b) of the Exchange Act.*

STO launch and legal considerations

To comply with the legal requirements of US securities laws, an issuer needs to consider the following:

- White paper—whether the content shows that this is an offering for digital tokens that would be considered as an investment contract under the Howey test
- Issuance of tokens—the number of tokens, the price, whether they are backed by assets/profits, and so on
- How the issuer markets the tokens
- Purchasers of the tokens
- Purchasers' expectations
- Use of tokens
- Whether there is a secondary market for the digital tokens

Summary

To issue an STO, issuers need to follow requirements under the Securities Act of 1933 and be monitored by the SEC and FinCEN. For state issuance, issuers are subject to the state's blue sky laws and state regulators. The main issue is that the federal and state governments' goals are to protect the general public and investors against fraud and ensure that the investors are informed so they can make informed investment decisions.

However, whether an STO is subject to US securities laws is very fact specific. As you can see from the preceding real cases, the SEC's analysis emphasizes the economic reality of the transaction and the way the creators of the tokens market the STO. The SEC will look at substance rather than form. A token being called a *utility token* will not preclude the SEC from reclassifying such a token as a security.

Other than securities law issues, an STO may also be subject to other laws or regulations, such as contract law, which governs the basic terms of the transaction and consumer law, torts, and so on if there are frauds or misrepresentations in the STO process that doesn't involve offerings in securities.

In Chapter 4, *Stablecoin,* we will cover the concepts of cryptocurrency and stablecoin and the challenges faced by stablecoin.

4
Stablecoin

Money, as a medium of exchange, has existed for thousands of years. It plays a critical role in economic activities. Money holds the characteristics of divisibility, durability, limited supply, portability, uniformity, and acceptability. Precious metals such as gold and silver satisfy these characteristics. Therefore, gold and silver are often used as money. Gold and silver have intrinsic values. For example, gold can be used to make jewelry. However, gold and silver as money have drawbacks. For instance, it is not convenient to carry a bag of gold when a trade involves a large amount of money. To address this issue (along with others), paper money was introduced and used. Unlike gold money, paper money does not have an intrinsic value. It has value, since an institution such as the government or a bank backs it.

Many people heard about blockchain technology because of currencies in a digital form with encryption—**cryptocurrencies**. Prices of cryptocurrencies are too volatile. Hence, they are not widely accepted, unlike fiat currencies, and fail to play a meaningful role in economic activities of the real world. Stablecoins were developed to resolve the price instability issue. They have become more popular since 2018, due to the dramatic falling of major cryptocurrencies, such as BTC, ETH, and XRP, in price. Stablecoin will perhaps make blockchain technology more relevant in economic activities. Currently, the stablecoin with the biggest market cap is **tether**, which is pegged to USD with an exchange rate of 1:1.

In this chapter, we will talk about the definition of money along with its basics. We will then proceed to the discussion on the concepts of cryptocurrency and stablecoin. We will explain the rationale behind the implementation of stablecoins and discuss types of stablecoins. At the end of the chapter, we will point out the challenges faced by stablecoin.

More specifically, the following topics are covered in this chapter:

- Basics of money
- Basics of stablecoin

Basics of money

Before money was introduced, people relied on bartering to acquire services and goods. Bartering is not an efficient way of trading goods and services, as it relies on luck to find a good match among the trading parties. To overcome this issue, items that were useful to everybody, such as cattle, sheep, vegetables, and grain were used as the medium of exchange. Suppose a fisherman needs to see a doctor. The fisherman can first go to a market and sell fish for cattle. Then, the fisherman brings the cattle to the doctor's practice to pay for healthcare services.

Using cattle as a medium of exchange is not ideal. In the preceding example, after having sold the fish, the fisherman may not immediately need a doctor's services and may not need to buy other goods. The fisherman has to feed the cattle and keep them alive for future payments. Given that the fisherman's expertise is not in rearing livestock, it is hard for him to ensure the cattle stay healthy. If the cattle die, then the cattle's value is reduced, and their remaining value is to be used as a source of food. Besides, cattle are not a scalable solution either. To tackle the problem, a new form of money such as gold was introduced to serve as a method of payment.

As humanity's economic activities increases, money has evolved. Fiat currencies were introduced and are widely used. A more recent development, as we have mentioned, is the introduction of cryptocurrency. The following is a list of several historical events that cover the evolution of money:

- **9000 – 6000 BC**: Cattle are the oldest form of money.
- **1200 BC**: Cowrie shells were first used in China as money and later in many other parts of the world.
- **1000 BC**: Shell-shaped bronze and copper coins, which are thought to be the earliest metal money, were made in China at the end of the stone age.
- **600 BC**: Outside China, the first known money was minted by King Alyattes in Lydia (today, part of Turkey) in 600 BC.
- **118 BC**: The first type of documented banknote was made and used in China. It was made of pieces of white deerskin and one-foot square in size. This is essentially the leather money that could be thought of being a predecessor to paper money.
- **Around 806 AD**: China became the first country to use paper banknotes.

- **1816 – 1930s AD**: In 1816, England officially made gold the standard of value, marking the start of the Gold Standard age. The Great Depression of the 1930s marked the beginning of the end of the Gold Standard age.
- **2008 AD**: The Bitcoin platform went live, marking the introduction of cryptocurrencies.

What is money?

Money refers to any medium of exchange in circulation, which includes coins, paper bills, banknotes, deposits in a bank account, and so on. It is used as a method of payment for goods and services. A person's wealth is measured in the amount of money that person owns.

Money's primary functions are as follows:

- **A medium of exchange**: Money is used for facilitating the exchanges of goods and services. It performs the function as a medium of exchange. Any goods or services can be exchanged for money. Conversely, people can pay money in exchange for goods or services. Money, as a medium of exchange, avoids the inefficiencies of a bartering system, which has issues such as coincidence-matching of needs. (In a bartering system, goods and services being traded have to be needed by both parties in order to make a trade feasible. This is often not the case and has to rely on luck. In other words, such a matching is coincident). Although money plays the role as a medium, it cannot affect the employment or income of a nation.
- **A unit of account**: Money is a method of comparing the value of dissimilar objects. It is used as a common denomination for measuring goods and services. The value of goods or services is expressed or measured in units of money, for example, $1 or $10. Similarly, the amount involved in financial activities or economic transactions, such as taking out a loan or the importing/exporting of goods, is represented in units of money. Thanks to this function of money, the value of assets, commodities, or services can be compared, and their exchange ratios can be determined conveniently.

Secondary functions of money include the following:

- **A store of value**: The value of goods or commodities, for example, fruits, vegetables, or meat, can be short-lived. To preserve their value, goods or commodities can be exchanged for money. Later, the money can be used to purchase similar goods or commodities. Hence, money plays the function of storing the value of the goods or commodities. To function well, the value of money should be relatively stable, for example, no hyperinflation. Furthermore, money should have the features of being saved or stored conveniently and retrieved easily for future payments.
- **Standard of deferred payments**: In modern society, people can rely on credit to purchase goods or pay for services, such as credit cards or taking out a loan, and so on. In other words, a customer purchases an item now and pays later, or borrows now and repays in the future. In these scenarios, money serves as a standard of deferred payments, which is accepted as a way to settle a debt. Essentially, money plays the role as a legal tender for repayment of debt.
- **Transfer of money**: Regardless of location and time, money can be transferred from one person to another. Money can be moved from one place to another.

Additional functions of money include the following:

- Measurement and distribution of national income
- Basis of credit
- Storing/saving purchasing power
- Providing liquidity

In general, any item that satisfies the three functions of a medium of exchange, a store of value, and a measure of value can be considered *money*. Money has different forms, for example, physical items, coins, banknotes, bank deposits, digital currency, and so on.

Money can be classified into four types:

- **Commodity money**: This is the oldest type of money. Examples are gold, silver, beads, cowrie shells, spices, and so on.
- **Fiat currency**: This is money that is decreed by the government to be legal tender. Fiat currency is not backed as a physical asset. The government mandates its value, which is agreed by parties involved in an exchange. Fiat currency is circulated in the form of metal coins or paper bills. The central bank (most of the time) or the Department of the Treasury (sometimes) of a country holds the responsibility of minting the coins and printing bills.

- **Commercial bank money**: Both central and commercial banks can create money. The money created by a central bank is the **base money**, and the one created by a commercial bank is the **commercial bank money**. By purchasing assets or lending money to banks, the central bank injects base money into the economy. By using the loaned money from the central bank, commercial banks create credits for being lent to clients through the fractional reserve banking approach. The term **fractional reserve banking** refers to the process of a commercial bank taking the deposited money (from the central bank or customers) minus the minimum reserve amount. The resulting amount is the amount of new credits that the bank can create. Here, the **minimal reserve amount** is expressed in the percentage of total deposits, which is called the **reserve ratio**, for example, 10%. The central bank sets the actual figure of the reserve ratio. The central bank can adjust the supply of commercial bank money by increasing or decreasing the reserve ratio. The newly issued credit is called the **commercial bank money** or **credit money**, since a portion of the new money being lent out may return to the banks, which are available for the creation of additional credit money. This iterative creation of money that does not previously exist is called the **money multiplier effect**. Therefore, the total amount of bank money is multiple factors of the original base money. This factor is called the **multiplier factor**. Roughly, the multiplier factor is around 10. In other words, when a central bank issues $1 base money, it effectively injects $10 into the economy. The money created by either a central bank or a commercial bank is equal. They are interchangeable.
- **Fiduciary money**: This is not mandated by the government, and is, therefore, not legally required to be accepted as a means of payment. Its value comes from the confidence on the issuer's promise that, upon request, a bearer will be paid by the issuer in fiat currency or commodity money. Checks, banknotes, and drafts are examples of fiduciary money.

Characteristics of money

Money possess six important characteristics:

- Durability
- Portability
- Divisibility
- Uniformity
- Limited supply
- Acceptability

Durability

The **durability** of money includes both the physical and social/institutional durability. Physical durability means the money being used repeatedly for a long time without deterioration, decomposition, wearing-out, or a change in its shape. Since money is a medium of exchange, it is used in circulation and will be physically passed around among trading parties. Physical durability is important so that the money keeps its value and stays in a usable state. Commodity money such as gold or cowrie shells is very durable. They can be used for a long time without damage. Cattle are only relatively durable because cattle can get sick or die. Paper money is durable as well but can wear out after being in circulation for a while. However, a worn-out paper bill can be easily replaced with a new one. Digital money is very durable. It exists as long as the platform that supports it is up and running.

Social and institutional durability refers to the durability of social institutions, for example, banks and governments. They are important, as the value of fiat or fiduciary money depends on the confidence in the existence of these institutions. If a government is overthrown or ceases to exist, it depends on whether a new government honors the old currency. If the new government does not honor the old currency, its value disappears totally. This happened in some countries where revolutions broke out and the old government was thrown out. Subsequently, the old fiat currency was abolished by the new government.

Similarly, fiduciary money depends on the issuing bank's ability to pay the bearer when it is requested. If a bank no longer exists, the bearer will not be able to redeem checks or bank notes unless another bank or the government steps in. Therefore, the perception of the durability of the institutions determines whether the fiat or fiduciary money is accepted.

Portability

Portability refers to whether money can be easily carried or moved from one place to another. As a medium of exchange and a means of payment, portability is an important characteristic of money. People travel and money is transferred from one person to another. Hence, money should be easily transferable among parties or can be conveniently moved from one location to another. Cattle are not easily moved, particularly over a long distance. In this sense, cattle are not good commodity money. Precious metals are portable, particularly when the amount is not very large. When a trade involves a large amount of money, commodity money is not as convenient as paper money. Paper money is much lighter and easily carried. A person can easily put a pile of $100 bills in a wallet, then travel and shop at various locations. It is not convenient to carry an equal amount of silver coins, which can weigh several pounds.

As online transactions become more widely available, many transactions are executed electronically. Along with this, money is exchanged electronically, and no physical money is required to be moved from one place to another. A cryptocurrency does not have a physical form. Cryptocurrencies-based transactions are completed virtually only. Cryptocurrencies are borderless, and they are global currencies. In other words, as long as they are being accepted, cryptocurrencies offer the best portability.

Divisibility

Divisibility refers to the money that can be easily divided or exchanged into smaller units for facilitating transactions. Imagine a person carries a silver bar weighing one pound and walks into a shop to buy a bag of bread. Suppose the bread is worth 0.1 pounds of silver. To complete a transaction, the shop owner should give 0.9 pounds of silver along with a bag of bread to the customer in exchange for the one-pound silver bar. Now, assume the silver bar is not divisible, and the shop owner offers ten bags of bread instead. It is less likely that the customer will accept the offer, since the customer only needs one bag, not ten bags of bread. Therefore, money needs to be divisible so that similar transactions can be facilitated.

Cattle or shells cannot be divided. A big cow or shell cannot be easily exchanged with smaller cows or shells. Therefore, they are not good commodity money. Gold or silver in its raw form achieves divisibility via having pieces with different weights. Governments manufacture gold and silver coins in various sizes and weights so that big coins can be changed to smaller coins easily. Paper bills have different denominations. They can be easily converted from one denomination into another.

Similarly, ETH and cryptocurrency have different denominations. BTC of bitcoin does not have different denominations. Instead, a BTC can be split into fractions, up to eight decimal points, providing sufficient divisibility to support real-world transactions.

Uniformity

Uniformity or **fungibility** refers to the standardization of money. For example, every $1 bill looks the same and is identical to another in value. A person holding one bill can exchange it for another bill of the same denomination without a change in its stored value. In other words, these $1 bills are fungible. No two cows or shells are identical. Precious-metal coins and paper money can be made perfectly equal in shape, size, or weight for satisfying the uniformity requirement. Cryptocurrencies satisfy the uniformity property perfectly.

Limited supply

Limited supply refers to the total supply of money, and it's limited. Money is valuable only when its supply is restricted. For example, counterfeits or the government printing a lot of paper money will lead to a currency's value decreasing. People's confidence in the money decreases and they will be less willing to accept the paper money to guard the value of their goods. In the old days, supplies of cattle and shells were considered to be relatively limited. The amount of precious metals such as gold on earth is limited. Excluding the normal use of gold, the remaining amount of gold available for making gold coins is, therefore, limited. But this may change. As humans make progress in technology, someday, it may become commercially viable to mine on a gold-rich planet. When this happens, the value of gold will drop significantly. In this case, the property of scarcity is violated, and gold will lose its status as money. The government determines the supply of fiat money. To maintain the stability of the value represented by the fiat currency, the government tightly controls the total supply of the currency. When encountering an economic hardship such as a recession or depression, a central bank tends to relax the money supply, which results in the printing of new paper money to rescue the country's economy. A downside of this practice is the reduction of value in fiat currency, leading to a so-called inflation (in the worst cases, hyperinflation) issue.

Cryptocurrencies, on the other hand, have a predefined total number of coins in supply at the time when a cryptocurrency is launched. For instance, BTC is set to have a limit of 21 million mineable coins. ETH initially did not have a cap on its total of coins, which led to concerns regarding inflation. An Ethereum project was later worked on to limit its supply. Although, for a given cryptocurrency, the supply of coins is limited, there is no limit in the total number of cryptocurrencies that can be created. Currently (as of February 3, 2019, `https://coinmarketcap.com/`), 2,104 cryptocurrencies are being issued and traded at cryptocurrency exchanges. This number increases as time passes.

Acceptability

General acceptability refers to the fact that money must be accepted by any person who provides goods and services to others. Cattle and gold are accepted widely. Paper money is accepted as long as the confidence in the government remains intact. Presently, the acceptance of cryptocurrency is limited. Some vendors accept BTC for payments. However, compared to the whole economy, the number of these vendors is tiny. Because of this, a cryptocurrency does not function the same way as a fiat currency does in real economies. People need to convert a cryptocurrency into fiat money in order to spend it in the real world.

Commodity money versus fiat currency

The terms *money* and *currency* are used interchangeably. However, they have some differences. The meaning of *money* is more generic. Currency is a *type* of money. For example, we often use *currency* when referring to fiat currencies. Commodity money is another type of money. There are differences between fiat currency and commodity money. One difference lies in how value is stored or derived for them. To explain the difference, we need to talk about *the value of money* first.

Money has two kinds of value: the **relative** value and the **absolute** value. The **relative value of money** refers to the purchasing power of money that can be used to buy goods and services. For example, a Big Mac costs different amounts at various cities in the US; the same Big Mac is more expensive in a big city such as New York City than in a small city located in a less affluent area. Even in the same location, a Big Mac cost less ten years ago than now. In other words, when we talk about the purchasing power of $1, its value is relative. One USD might have bought a Big Mac ten years ago, but now it can only buy half of the same Big Mac. In terms of purchasing a Big Mac, the value of $1 today is only half of its value 10 years ago. Here, the term **purchasing power** refers to the value of a currency expressed as how many goods or services can be bought with one unit of money.

The **absolute value of money** is also called the **intrinsic value of money**. It refers to the **use value** of the money as a commodity. For example, gold is used in electronic devices for connecting wires, thanks to its high efficiency for conducting currents. Electronic components made with gold are very reliable. The intrinsic value of money is determined by supply and demand. In the case of a cattle, when not being used as a medium of exchange, they can be treated as a source of meat for feeding people. The cattle's intrinsic value is the price that other people are willing to pay for its meat. For precious metal coins, such as gold, their absolute or intricate value is the raw material value when coins are melted. Normally, the intrinsic value of commodity money should not be higher than its denomination or face value. If this is not the case, people will take the money off the market and melt coins to sell them as raw materials for a profit, a process called **arbitrage**. The arbitrage process will quickly bring down its intrinsic value to a level that is the same as or less than the face value.

So, what are the differences between a fiat currency and commodity money—the real differences between them are that commodity money has both a relative and an absolute value, while a fiat currency has only a relative value. When a USD bill with a face value of $100 is treated purely as a piece of paper, it barely has any value. A gold coin when melted down is still worth something. If the fiat currency is pegged to gold, its value is not from the paper bill itself. It is from the underlying asset, the gold.

Consequently, commodity money and fiat currency fulfil the function of storing the value in different ways. Commodity money derives its value largely from its intrinsic value. Fiat currency drives the value from the fact that the government backs it. Similarly, fiduciary money and commercial bank money have a relative value only.

Since fiat currency does not have an intrinsic value, it faces the **inflation** problem. Inflation occurs when the units of money increase concerning the same units of goods and services. Suppose within a specific economy, originally, there are 100 million units of currency chasing after 100 million units of goods and services, that is, one unit of the fiat currency for one unit of goods/services. Suppose ten years later, the units of currency have been increased to 200 mm, while units of goods and services remain at 100 mm. Now 200 mm units of currency chase after 100 mm units of goods/services.

Consequently, it requires two units of currency to buy one unit of goods/services. The currency's purchasing power is only half of what it used to be 10 years ago. Everything else being equal, inflation decreases the purchasing power of the currency by 50%. Commodity money does not have the inflation issue unless its supply is increased dramatically due to the discovery of a large mining field or from an extra-terrestrial object. On the other hand, inflation will happen when the government prints new paper bills without the corresponding goods or services. If too many new paper bills are printed within a short period, it will lead to hyperinflation, making that money worthless overnight.

Currently, there are 180 fiat currencies worldwide. The British pound, GBP, is the world's oldest fiat currency and USD is the most widely used fiat currency. Some of the fiat currencies can be converted freely into each other and others cannot. The supply-and-demand rule at open markets determines the pair-wise conversion or exchange rate. Sometimes, for serving its economic goals, the central bank of a country intervenes for maintaining exchange rates within a targeted range via open market operations. In this case, the exchange rate may not reflect the true value of that country's currency. In this case, **Purchasing Power Parity** (**PPP**) can be used as an alternative way to measure the currency's true value. PPP uses a basket of goods and compares the prices in different countries. If the basket of goods is priced the same in the two countries, then the fiat currencies of these two countries are on a par or in equilibrium. The purchasing power-based exchange rate equals to the reciprocals of their price levels in the two countries.

An example of a fiat currency– the USD

The governments issue fiat currencies in the world. USD, the EUR, JPY, GBP, CND, CHF, CNY, and AUD are among the most frequently traded currencies. USD is the most in-demand fiat currency in the world. As of January 23, 2019, there are around 1.7 trillion USD in supply. USD is used by central banks to be the main reserve currency. In 2017, 62.7% of foreign-exchange reserves were in USD.

In comparison, the second place is the EUR at 21.15% followed by JPY at 4.89%. USD is also the designated currency for commodity trading such as crude oil and most of the international financial transactions. Therefore, USD plays the most important role in the world's economic and financial activities.

The roots of USD can be traced back to 244 years ago when the Continental Congress in 1775 decreed the issuance of Continental Currency. Treasury Secretary Salmon Chase in 1861 printed the first paper bill of USD. In 1834, the US moved to the Gold Standard by pegging USD to gold at $20.67 per Troy ounce; this made one dollar at 1.5 grams of gold. Meanwhile, USD had been pegged to other precious metals such as silver. In 1900, the **Gold Standard Act**, signed into law by President William McKinley, made gold the only standard for the dollar. In 1933, to deal with the bank run that led to the gold run—bank customers rushed to banks, converting paper dollars into gold. President Roosevelt ended the domestic dollar pegging to gold. In 1944, the Bretton Woods agreement signed by delegates from 44 allied countries assured the international arrangement of USD convertibility on demand to gold and other currency pegging to USD. In 1971, President Nixon unilaterally abolished the international convertibility of the USD into gold. Essentially, USD ended its Gold Standard. This was a significant event. When being pegged to gold, the units of USD that can be created and put into circulation have to be backed by the corresponding amount of gold in reserve. With the pegging to gold being dismantled, the US government can print additional paper money freely.

Basics of stablecoin

In the previous section, we introduced the basics of money, which can be either commodity money or fiat money. Now we are ready to talk about stablecoin in this section. Before getting to this main topic of this chapter, we must first talk about cryptocurrency.

Cryptocurrency

A cryptocurrency is a currency in a digital form with encryption. In other words, it is a digital asset used as a medium of exchange. Bitcoin is considered to be the first cryptocurrency, whose platform initially went live in early 2009. It is based on the proposal in the white paper circulated by Satoshi Nakamoto in October 2008. Since then, cryptocurrencies receive immense attention. New cryptocurrencies were created and issued. At the moment, over 2,100 (2,106, to be exact, on February 5, 2019, see `https://coinmarketcap.com/`) cryptocurrencies are traded at cryptocurrency exchanges. The top three market-cap cryptocurrencies are **bitcoin (BTC)**, **Ripple (XRP)**, and **Ethereum (ETH)**. BTC is the dominant cryptocurrency. XRP and ETH vie for second place.

Before BTC, work on the creation of a digital form of currency with cryptography had already been started years earlier. Here are samples of past important work in this area:

- In 1982, David Chaum proposed **e-cash**, anonymous electronic money with encryption. His idea was implemented in 1995.
- In 1996, the **National Security Agency (NSA)** published a paper entitled *How to Make a Mint: the Cryptography of Anonymous Electronic Cash*, describing a cryptocurrency design.
- In 1998, Wei Dai published the protocol for **b-money**, an anonymous, distributed electronic cash system. B-money is considered to be a predecessor of BTC. Satoshi Nakamoto referred to it while describing BTC.
- In 1998, Nick Szabo architectured **bit gold**, a decentralized digital currency. Although bit gold was never implemented, it is thought to be architecturally a predecessor of BTC.
- In 2004, Hal Finney adapted the concept of **proof of work (PoW)** to money by using the idea of reusable proof of work. He continued the work of Dai and implemented a cryptocurrency system.

Many of the cryptocurrencies in existence do not have a real use, except for being speculated. However, a few of them are put into real use. For example, Ripple Labs Inc. has built Ripple, a currency exchange and remittance network. It is a real-time settlement platform. Its native cryptocurrency is XRP. In Q4 of 2018, Ripple's product, **xRapid**, went live and became commercially available. xRapid uses XRP to facilitate cross-border transactions. The largest US bank in market cap, JP Morgan, in February of 2019, announced a rival coin—**JPM Coin**. (JPM Coin is a stablecoin.)

One issue that hinders the wide adoption of cryptocurrency in real applications is the high volatility in its price. The price change of BTC in 2017 and 2018 is jaw-dropping. XRP's price change is equally volatile. You can visit `https://coinmarketcap.com/` to check the price changes of XRP. From the site, you can see XRP's price was $0.25 on December 8. 2017. It reached the peak price of $3.65 on January 4, 2018 (a 1,360% increase in less than a month). Then, XRP's price reached a low point of $0.49 on April 11, 2018.

The issue of high volatility in price can be explained with a hypothetical example. Suppose a person working in the US wants to use Ripple's xRapid for transferring 1,000 hard-earned USDs to his wife living in another country. To do so, the $1,000 will first be converted into the corresponding amount of XRP, which is then sent to his wife's country on the xRapid platform. Upon completion of the operation, the XRP coins are converted into the local fiat currency. The time it takes Ripple's platform to complete the cross-border move is around 3 – 5 seconds. The cost is only a fraction of the price charged by a bank using a traditional method. However, the end-to-end time (between the husband paying in USD, and the wife receiving the money in the local currency) may take longer. The actual time will depend on the liquidity of the cryptocurrency markets where the conversions (USD into XRP and then XRP into the local currency) take place. If the XRP price drops by 1% during that time, the customer will lose equivalently $10, which may be higher than the transaction cost charged by Ripple. With the possibility of losing money due to high volatility in the cryptocurrency price, it will not be easy to convince ordinary customers to use the application for transferring money. (Of course, this is only a hypothetical example for illustration purposes. In reality, Ripple's xRapid perhaps has already worked out a solution to address the issue. In the case of the JP Morgan solution, JMP Coin is issued to be a stablecoin for tackling the problem).

The hypothetical example reveals a deficiency of cryptocurrencies—lack of stability or poorness in storing a value. Unlike a fiat/fiduciary money, which is backed by the government or an issuer, there is no institution backing the cryptocurrencies. (This could change in future, for example, if central banks issue fiat cryptocurrencies). The price of these cryptocurrencies is completely determined by the supply-and-demand rule of markets. Hence, the value of cryptocurrencies is not stable. Workers will unlikely accept paychecks in the form of BTC coins when they are not sure whether the coins will be worth the same, at the time, to pay mortgages, food, or medical bills. Stablecoins are introduced to address the stability issue.

What are stablecoins?

Stablecoins refers to a set of cryptocurrencies that are designed to hold stable values. The stability of their value is achieved by pegging the price to other types of money such as commodity money, for example, gold, or a fiat currency such as USD.

The first stablecoin, **bitUSD**, was introduced and implemented by BitShares on July 21, 2014. bitUSD is a token on the BitShares blockchain. The BitShares blockchain has its native cryptocurrency, **BTS**. (An analogy is the native cryptocurrency ETH on the Ethereum blockchain platform with an ERC-20 token issued as a stablecoin). bitUSD is pegged to USD with a face value, $1, and can be traded freely on BitShares. It provides services covering a decentralized exchange to smart contract-managed payments. One bitUSD token is collateralized with $2 in BTS, which is an example of the stablecoin type called **crypto-collateralized**. Here, the collateralizing amount, $2, instead of $1, is used for compensating the high volatility in the BTS price.

Although being introduced as the first stablecoin, bitUSD is not the most popular stablecoin. Currently, **tether** (**USDT**) is the stablecoin leading in the market cap. Tether was launched on October 3, 2014. Like bitUSD, tether is pegged to USD. However, they differ in two key areas. First, USDT is a native cryptocurrency on its blockchain platform, not just a token. Second, USDT is collateralized by USD, not a cryptocurrency. A USDT can be issued when $1 is deposited into a bank account. In other words, only when a USD is taken out of circulation can a USDT be minted. Thanks to the pegging, the price of USDT is stable at around 1 USD, as you can check at `https://coinmarketcap.com/`. In comparison, the price of BTS is not stable at all, since BTS is a non-stablecoin cryptocurrency.

In response to the dramatic decrease in the price of major cryptocurrencies, stablecoins have significantly gained popularity since 2018. Investments, for example, from crypto-specific venture capital funds are poured on new stablecoin projects. The number of stablecoins has doubled. Besides USDT and bitUSD, other stablecoins include MakerDAO's Dai, Basecoin, Basis, Saga, **TrueUSD** (**TUSD**), **Paxos Standard** (**PAX**), **CENTRE**, **Gemini dollar** (**GUSD**), Bitcoin Air (USDAP), **Digix Gold Tokens** (**DGX**), and so on. In 2018, the top stablecoins were as follows:

- Tether (USDT)
- MakerDAO (Dai)
- TUSD
- Carbon
- Kowala

- cryptopeg
- Boreal
- Basecoin
- bitUSD
- NuBits

Stablecoins have several advantages. Here are a few of them:

- Customers are more willing to accept and use stablecoins as a medium of exchange to pay for goods and services.
- Many cryptocurrency projects are for speculation rather than changing the real-world economies. Stablecoins are different. They can help blockchain technology to realize its true value and unlock the benefits of decentralization networks.
- Stablecoins can become global currencies, that is, play the role as a global medium of exchange. If achieved, it has several advantages such as helping countries with unstable currencies or reducing cross-border transaction costs due to the elimination of FX costs.
- Stablecoin can support decentralized financial services, such as cross-border financing or lending. This type of borderless service has become feasible and cheaper.

Are stablecoins really stable?

One constant criticism of stablecoin is the word *stable*. Critics of stablecoins point out that no coin is stable, even being pegged to gold or a fiat currency. In absolute terms, this statement is true.

For example, the gold price has experienced a wide ride over the years. The chart at Macrotrends (https://www.macrotrends.net/1333/historical-gold-prices-100-year-chart) displays the historical (**Consumer Price Index** (**CPI**) inflation-adjusted) gold prices per ounce from January of 1915 to January of 2019. During the period, the highest gold price reached was $2,189.17 (CPI adjusted, January 1, 1980) per ounce, and the lowest was $230.77 (December 1, 1970). On February 8, 2019, the gold price was $1,311.10 per ounce. In conclusion, the price of gold is not stable.

A fiat currency such as USD is highly volatile too. By checking the USD FX plots at Macrotrends (`https://www.macrotrends.net/charts/exchange-rates`), you can find the values of the **US Dollar Index** (**USDX**) in the past 43 years. Here, the USDX refers to a measure of the USD value in relation to a basket of US trading partners' currencies. The index goes up if USD is more valuable than its partners' currencies, or vice versa. The chart has a high value of 128 (February of 1985) and a low value of 80 (July of 2011). Similarly, other major fiat currencies such as the EUR, GBP, or JPY are equally, or even more volatile.

In summary, when we talk about the stability of a stablecoin, we only talk in relative terms. For example, if a stablecoin price is pegged to USD, we say this stablecoin is stable in USD only. Although the stability of a stablecoin is relative, it is still very useful. By pegging to the price of a fiat or commodity money (instead of to the price of a cryptocurrency), a stablecoin removes the correlated volatility within the ecosystem of the blockchain. For illustration purposes, suppose a stablecoin price is pegged to the native cryptocurrency of its blockchain platform. Then, the price of this stablecoin varies in correlation to the price of the cryptocurrency. That is, their prices move up or down concurrently. On the other hand, if a stablecoin is pegged to USD, then its price change will be irrelevant to the price change of the corresponding cryptocurrency. Since the volatility of a cryptocurrency is much higher than that of gold money or a fiat currency such as USD, EUR, GBP, and so on, the stablecoin price is relatively stable.

Types of stablecoins

Stablecoins are classified into several types. They can be collateralized and uncollateralized. Within the collateralized type, they can be commodity-collateralized, fiat-collateralized, or crypto-collateralized. All types have pros and cons. Before proceeding to the detailed discussions on each type of stablecoin, we first explain the differences between peg and collateralization.

Peg refers to one country's currency being pegged to that of another country with a stable economy by fixing the exchange rate. There are, in general, four types of peg:

- Crawling peg
- Adjustable peg
- Basket peg
- Commodity peg

A **crawling peg** refers to a process of exchange-rate adjustments that allow depreciation or appreciation to happen gradually. The exchange rate fluctuates within a permitted range around a pegged rate. The pegged rate is adjusted gradually until it reaches a target rate. For example, during the 1990s, the Mexican government adopted the crawling peg method to devalue the Peso against the USD until reaching an acceptable rate.

An **adjustable peg** refers to a fixed exchange rate to a major currency such as the USD or the EUR with built-in flexibility of fluctuations. The fluctuation stays within a predefined range, say, 1–2%. If the rate variations go beyond this range, the central bank will intervene via open-market operations to bring the exchange rate back within the defined range of the pegged rate. Many Asian countries, for example, Indonesia, Malaysia, the Philippines, and South Korea have adopted this pegging type. Unlike the crawling peg, the pegged rate of the adjustable peg stays the same.

A **basket peg** refers to a currency being pegged to a weighted average of its main trading partners' currencies. A basket peg is for diversification, which makes the currency more stable. One example is the Chinese yuan, which is pegged to a basket of 24 currencies.

A **commodity peg** refers to a currency being pegged to a precious commodity, such as gold. For example, the gold standard, where a country's currency is pegged to gold, was widely used to stabilize currencies during the nineteenth and early twentieth century.

On the other side, **collateralization** refers to just that: a borrower pledges an asset to the lender as a surety to guarantee a debt being repaid in the future. If the borrower defaults on their obligations, the lender has the option to take over the collateralized asset. A mortgage is a well-known example where a client takes a loan to buy a house, which is used as collateral to reduce the lender's risk. If a customer defaults on payments, the lender can repossess the house and recuperate the residual loans via the process called **foreclosure**.

In the context of stablecoins, pegging refers to a stablecoin having a fixed conversion rate to or from a fiat currency or commodity money. Here, pegging does not necessarily involve collateral. When a stablecoin is collateralized by an asset, the asset is the collateral that backs the value of a stablecoin.

Commodity-collateralized stablecoins

The term **commodity-collateralized stablecoins** refers to stablecoins that are backed by commodity money such as gold. The underlying asset can be a single or a basket of commodities. Commodity-backed stablecoins tokenize the backing commodities on a blockchain. The commodity or commodities guarantee the value of stablecoins. Ownership of stablecoins represents a claim to the collateral. In other words, investors can exchange their stablecoins for its backing commodity based on a predefined conversion rate.

Advantages of commodity-collateralized stablecoins include the following: redeemable to tangible assets, the price of assets is relatively stable, and the liquidity of the underlying assets makes these coins liquid. There are disadvantages as well. They become centralized due to the collaterals being central. This is in contrary to the decentralization philosophy of the blockchain technology. Centralization has a single point of failure. Another disadvantage is that auditing could be expensive and time-consuming.

Fiat-collateralized stablecoins

Fiat-collateralized stablecoins refer to stablecoins fully backed by one or a basket of fiat currencies such as USD, EUR, or GBP, that is, a fiat-collateralized stablecoin is backed by real money being deposited in a bank account. If a stablecoin is pegged to USD, an investor pays $1 and receives a newly issued stablecoin. When the investor exchanges a unit of the stablecoin back into one USD, the stablecoin is destroyed, and the $1 deposited originally is returned to the investor. Advantages of fiat-collateralized stablecoins include that they are simple and easy to understand and the price is stable since governments back the pegged fiat currencies. They have a few disadvantages. For example, money paid to buy stablecoins is deposited at a centralized place. (A bank account is a centralized place.)

Consequently, they lost the feature of decentralization. Fiat-collateral stablecoins require trusts from investors, since enforcement of fiat currency collateralization relies on promises of the issuer, and not by a built-in mechanism. There is nothing to prevent a stablecoin issuer from minting more stablecoins than the promised 1:1 ratio. Also, the issuer can easily take the money and run away due to the centralized deposit set-up. Tether, the most well-known fiat-collateralized stablecoin, has been criticized constantly for lacking transparency on its USD holdings. Some critics have even questioned tether for issuing more stablecoins than the USD collaterals. Besides, a fiat currency requires greater oversight and regulations. These regulations can reduce the conversion efficiency between collateralized fiat currencies and the stablecoins.

Crypto-collateralized stablecoins

The term **crypto-collateralized stablecoins** refers to stablecoins being collateralized by one or a basket of cryptocurrencies such as BTC or ETH. One example is MakerDAO's stablecoin, Dai. Dai is an ERC-20 token and is pegged to USD with a ratio of 1:1. Although being pegged to USD, Dai is not collateralized by USD. In other words, when a Dai token is issued, no $1 is required to be deposited into a bank account. The pegging to $1 is achieved through a component consisting of smart contracts—**Collateralized Debt Position (CDP)**. CDP responds to price fluctuations and adjusts the Dai price automatically.

By moving away from being collateralized by commodity or fiat money, the crypto-collateralized stablecoins maintain the decentralization implementation and keep the efficiency in conversions. The efficiency in conversion is gained due to no fiat currency-related regulations being required, as crypto-collateralized stablecoins do not involve a fiat currency. It provides transparency too, since all transactions are available on the blockchain. Their main issue is that the cryptocurrency price is highly volatile. Therefore, the value of the collateral fluctuates highly. Taking a haircut is one way to address it. For example, for the crypto-collateralized stablecoin, bitUSD, every $2 of BTS is required as collateral for $1 of a bitUSD token. In this case, 50% of the haircut is taken on the value of the collateralizing cryptocurrency. The downside is that an investor may be reluctant to pay two dollar's worth of cryptocurrency in exchange for one dollar's worth of stablecoin. Another issue is the implementation of a crypto-backed stablecoin, which involves complicated algorithms.

Non-collateralized stablecoins

The term **non-collateralized stablecoins** refers to stablecoins whose price is pegged to a fiat currency 1:1, and which are not backed by collateral. Per quantity theory of money, the general price changes of currency are related proportionally to the changes in the money supply. A central bank maintains the stability of its fiat currency by either increasing or reducing the supply of the currency. A common method to implement non-collateralized stablecoins is called the **seigniorage shares approach**. The idea is to mimic the approach of a central bank by creating a central crypto-bank. Supply of the stablecoins will be adjusted algorithmically using smart contracts in a decentralized manner. If the price of a stablecoin is above the pegged value, the supply increases. If the price is less than the pegged value, the supply decreases. One example is **Basecoin**. It was issued as an ERC-20 token on Ethereum. At the time when it was launched, Basecoin was pegged to USD 1:1. Later, the pegging can be expanded to a basket of assets or an index such as CPI. Basecoin was subsequently renamed to **Basis**. Advantages of non-collateralized stablecoins are decentralization, the absence of collaterals, and price stability. The biggest disadvantage is the complexity in implementation.

An alternative way to categorize stablecoins is to divide them into centralized stablecoins and decentralized stablecoins. Commodity- and fiat-collateralized stablecoins are the **centralized stablecoins**. Crypto-collateralized and non-collateralized stablecoins are **decentralized stablecoins**.

Challenges of stablecoins

Although stablecoins have gained popularity since 2018, they face challenges that need to be dealt with.

Stablecoins are not fully tested in real-world economies. The effectiveness of their economics is yet to be discovered. The stability of a stablecoin is achieved via pegging its price to one or a basket of currencies. Hence, stablecoin is like a fiat currency that adopts to the fixed exchange rate regime. As a result, stablecoins suffer the same drawbacks. For example, for a fixed exchange rate fiat currency, it is expensive to maintain the fixed rate, since the central bank of a country needs to keep sufficient reserves of the pegged fiat currency. Furthermore, when the country's economy is in bad shape, its currency will be more likely attacked by speculators. This is exactly what happened to several Asian currencies, for example, Thailand, during the Asian financial crisis (July 1997–December 1998).

Fiat- or commodity money-backed stablecoins lack an established auditing process to ensure the enforcement of the collateralization rules. This leaves a door open for human manipulations such as minting more stablecoins than the collaterals. In general, the centralized stablecoins face the risk of human errors or manipulations.

When a stablecoin is pegged to a fiat currency (or a basket of currencies), stablecoin suffers the same inflation issue along with its pegged fiat currency (or a basket of currencies). When the pegged currency loses the purchasing power, the stablecoin loses an equal amount of value because of the 1:1 pegging. Only when a stablecoin is pegged to commodity money is inflation not an issue.

For stablecoins backed by multi-assets, dropping in the value of one asset requires being compensated with an increase of an equal amount in another backing asset. If a sufficient number of backing assets lose their values, this can potentially cascade to a bank-run such as an issue demanding for a value increase on a concentrated set of backing assets.

Also, stablecoins can be prone to failure. The once high-flying stablecoin project Basis was shut down in December 2018. One cited reason was the concerns regarding US regulations. **NuBits** is another example of a failed stablecoin, since NuBits could not maintain its pegging.

Summary

In this chapter, we talked about the definition of money and its basics. We outlined types of money including commodity money, for example, gold; fiat currencies, for example, USD; fiduciary money, for example, bank-issued checks; and commercial bank money, for example, bank-issued credits.

The characteristics of money were discussed in detail. Money's six characteristics are divisibility, durability, limited supply, portability, uniformity, and acceptability. It was pointed out that commodity money has two types of value: the absolute (intrinsic) value and the relative value. Commodity money has both intrinsic and relative values. Fiat currency has only the relative value. Currently, there are 180 fiat currencies worldwide. USD is the most important fiat currency. It is widely used in international trading and financial activities. USD is the top reserve currency that central banks use to maintain their countries' foreign reserves.

A cryptocurrency is built on a blockchain platform. It is a currency in digital form with encryption. The price of cryptocurrencies is too volatile, an issue preventing cryptocurrency from being widely accepted in real economic activities. Stablecoins are developed to address the issue. Stablecoins can potentially unlock the true values of the blockchain technology and develop decentralization (or community) economies. The price of a stablecoin is pegged to a fiat currency or commodity money. Historically, the price of gold or fiat currency is not stable. Due to the pegging, the price of a stablecoin is, therefore, not stable. Hence, a stablecoin is stable only with its pegged fiat currency or commodity money. Stablecoins have two main types: collateralized and uncollateralized. For collateralized stablecoins, the collaterals can be either commodity assets, fiat currencies, or cryptocurrencies. Stablecoins are classified alternatively into centralized, for example, commodity- or fiat currency- backed and decentralized, such as cryptocurrency-backed or non-collateralized stablecoins. In the end, we pointed out some of the challenges faced by stablecoin.

In the next chapter, `Chapter 5`, *Security Token Smart Contracts,* we will talk about how to develop STO smart contracts on an Ethereum platform via the issuing of standard Ethereum ERC1400 tokens. We will show a use case of STO with working code.

Security Token Smart Contracts

5

In the previous chapters, we learned the core fundamental concepts of the security token and we also understood a lot about digital tokens under US security law.

Regulation is fundamental to the running of financial systems. It protects investors from the uncertainties of the markets and creates stability. Security tokens are designed to connect two very different worlds between blockchain smart contracts and regulated finance. Smart contracts can apply regulation rules on security tokens.

In this chapter, we will overview popular security token protocols and understand how regulation rules can be enforced at the smart contract level. We will also cover Ethereum smart contract basics—solidity programming. This chapter is organized around three major topics, as follows:

- ERC-20 and ERC-721 tokens
- Security token technical design overview
- Introduction to smart contracts

ERC-20 and ERC-721 token

In Ethereum, most tokens are used as digital currency and can be interchangeable like ERC-20 tokens, but other tokens such as ERC-721 are for collectables, which are not interchangeable. These types of token are called non-fungible tokens.

In this section, we will overview these two types of token. We will look at the smart contract interface and discuss functions defined in the interface.

ERC-20

ERC-20 is the most popular Ethereum blockchain technical standard for tokens that are issued on Ethereum. It was proposed by Fabian Vogelsteller on November 19, 2015. ERC stands for **Ethereum Request for Comment**, and **20** is a unique ID number for the request to differentiate it from other standards. Currently, there are more than 65,000 ERC-20 tokens in existence, although many of these tokens have no market value.

The ERC-20 token defines the following common list of rules in the smart contract:

```
contract ERC20Interface {
    function totalSupply() public view returns (uint);
    function balanceOf(address tokenOwner) public view returns (uint
balance);
    function allowance(address tokenOwner, address spender) public view
returns (uint remaining);
    function transfer(address to, uint tokens) public returns (bool
success);
    function approve(address spender, uint tokens) public returns (bool
success);
    function transferFrom(address from, address to, uint tokens) public
returns (bool success);

    event Transfer(address indexed from, address indexed to, uint tokens);
    event Approval(address indexed tokenOwner, address indexed spender,
uint tokens);
}
```

The relevant functions are listed as follows:

- `totalSupply()`: Returns the total token supply.
- `balanceOf()`: Gets the balance of the account for the given address.
- `allowance()`: Returns the allowance amount from _owner.
- `transfer()`: Transfers the balance from the owner's account to another account and must fire the transfer event.
- `transferFrom()`: Sends the amount of tokens from `address from` to `address to`. The `transferFrom()` method is used to withdraw the workflow, allowing contracts to transfer tokens on your behalf.
- `approve()`: Allows the spender to withdraw from your account with a certain amount.

Before the ERC token standard, the numerous **initial coin offerings (ICOs)** start-ups or Dapps had created their own tokens with many different standards.

After the release of the ERC-20 standard, things changed and have become much more streamlined.

The benefits of ERC-20 tokens include the following:

- Reduces the risk of contract breaking
- Reduces the complexity of token interactions
- Uniform and quicker transactions
- Confirms transactions more efficiently
- Enhances token liquidity

However, ERC-20 tokens do not have regulatory built-in limitations by design, so there are no restrictions for transferring them. This kind of token is known as a utility token. When dealing with security regulations, token holders must apply for **know your customer (KYC)/anti-money laundering (AML)** verification processes; token trading is subject to federal security regulations and many additional constraints apply to these regulations.

Since the ERC-20 token is widely adopted in the industry, currently most of the security token ERC standard proposals are ERC-20-compatible, which means that potentially all wallets and exchanges supporting ERC-20 will support these tokens as well.

In ERC-20 standards, when a user trades these tokens, all of the token supply can be treated as the same value; it is interchangeable. The ERC-20 token is a **fungible token (FT)**. An FT is a core characteristic of cryptocurrencies. It can be easily replaced by something identical and it is interchangeable with ease, like bitcoin.

On the other hand, a **non-fungible token (NFT)** is a special type of cryptographic token that has unique information or attributes. NFTs are thus irreplaceable or not interchangeable. For this purpose, the ERC-721 token was created as a standard.

 Dieter Shirley, the creator of CryptoKitties, developed the term NFT.

Each token within the contract represents a different value. Let's take a look at the ERC-721 standard.

ERC-721 – NFTs

ERC-721 is an NFT standard, also known as deeds. ERC-721 was created in January 2018, proposed by William Entriken, Dieter Shirley, Jacob Evans, and Nastassia Sachs.

The best known example of ERC-721 is the CryptoKitties game. In the game, there are thousands of CryptoKitties. Each cat has unique genes, and owns a name, color, shape, price, and other profiles. The player can collect and breed adorable kittens. Each of CryptoKitties' collectable digital assets can be traded, sold, and bought by a player:

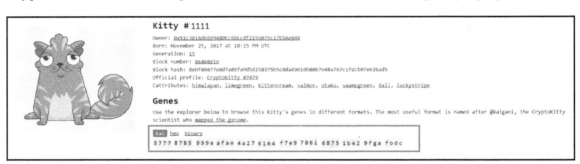

 ERC-721 became famous because of the success of CryptoKitties.

Let's look at the following `ERC721` interface:

```
interface ERC721 /* is ERC165 */ {
    event Transfer(address indexed _from, address indexed _to, uint256
indexed _tokenId);
    event Approval(address indexed _owner, address indexed _approved,
uint256 indexed _tokenId);
    event ApprovalForAll(address indexed _owner, address indexed _operator,
bool _approved);
    function balanceOf(address _owner) external view returns (uint256);
    function ownerOf(uint256 _tokenId) external view returns (address);
    function safeTransferFrom(address _from, address _to, uint256 _tokenId,
bytes data) external payable;
    function safeTransferFrom(address _from, address _to, uint256 _tokenId)
external payable;
    function transferFrom(address _from, address _to, uint256 _tokenId)
external payable;
    function approve(address _approved, uint256 _tokenId) external payable;
    function setApprovalForAll(address _operator, bool _approved) external;
```

```
    function getApproved(uint256 _tokenId) external view returns (address);
    function isApprovedForAll(address _owner, address _operator) external
view returns (bool);
}
interface ERC165 {
    function supportsInterface(bytes4 interfaceID) external view returns
(bool);
}
```

The functions are listed as follows:

- balanceOf: Finds the balance of an input address
- ownerOf: Returns the owner address for a given token ID
- safeTransferFrom: Transfers an NFT ownership from one address to another address, as opposed to transferFrom, and it also checks whether the recipient is a valid ERC-721 receiver address
- transferFrom: Transfers ownership of an NFT
- approve: Gives a given entity permission to transfer a token
- setApprovalForAll: Controls the approval for a third party (operator) to manage all of msg.sender assets
- getApproved: Gets the approved address for a single NFT
- isApprovedForAll: Checks if approve for all addresses is allowed

The NFT concept is adopted by many security tokens. In the following table, we list fungible and non-fungible types for some popular security token standards:

Token	Type
ERC-1400	NFT
ST-20	FT
Regulated Token (R-Token)	FT
ERC-1410	**partially fungible token (PFT)**

We have just overviewed the ERC-20 and ERC-721 tokens. In the next section, we will look into the current popular security token technical design.

Security token technical design overview

Security tokens, like ERC-20 tokens with built-in regulatory restrictions, protect investors' rights at the token level. It redefines the whole process through which companies or startups raise money.

As of today, many different standards are being proposed and implemented in the marketplace. In this section, we'll look into the following Ethereum security token standards:

- ERC-1400/ERC-1410
- ST-20
- R-Token
- SRC-20
- DS-Token
- ERC-1404
- ERC-884

ERC-1400/ERC-1410

The ERC-1410 PFT standard is part of the ERC-1400 security token standards. ERC-1410 was created in September, 2018, and proposed by Adam Dossa (@adamdossa), Pablo Ruiz (@pabloruiz55), Fabian Vogelsteller (@frozeman), and Stephane Gosselin (@thegostep). The current **Ethereum Improvement Proposal** (**EIP**) status is draft. ERC-1400/ERC- 1410 is being supported and implemented by Polymath.

A PFT allows the token contract to divide an owner's tokens into a set of partitions; some of these tokens are fungible, and others may not be fungible.

ERC-1410 provides a standard interface for grouping an owner's tokens into a set of partitions. On each partition, it represents the individual token identifying a key and a balance. This provides token holder transparency to track the overall supply of tokens and overall balance of owners.

The following is the ERC1410 token interface:

```
interface IERC1410 {
    // Token Information
    function balanceOf(address _tokenHolder) external view returns
(uint256);
    function balanceOfByPartition(bytes32 _partition, address _tokenHolder)
```

```
external view returns (uint256);
    function partitionsOf(address _tokenHolder) external view returns
(bytes32[]);
    function totalSupply() external view returns (uint256);
    // Token Transfers
    function transferByPartition(bytes32 _partition, address _to, uint256
_value, bytes _data) external returns (bytes32);
    function operatorTransferByPartition(bytes32 _partition, address _from,
address _to, uint256 _value, bytes _data, bytes _operatorData) external
returns (bytes32);
    function canTransferByPartition(address _from, address _to, bytes32
_partition, uint256 _value, bytes _data) external view returns (byte,
bytes32, bytes32);
    // Operator Information
    function isOperator(address _operator, address _tokenHolder) external
view returns (bool);
    function isOperatorForPartition(bytes32 _partition, address _operator,
address _tokenHolder) external view returns (bool);
    // Operator Management
    function authorizeOperator(address _operator) external;
    function revokeOperator(address _operator) external;
    function authorizeOperatorByPartition(bytes32 _partition, address
_operator) external;
    function revokeOperatorByPartition(bytes32 _partition, address
_operator) external;
    // Issuance / Redemption
    function issueByPartition(bytes32 _partition, address _tokenHolder,
uint256 _value, bytes _data) external;
    function redeemByPartition(bytes32 _partition, uint256 _value, bytes
_data) external;
    function operatorRedeemByPartition(bytes32 _partition, address
_tokenHolder, uint256 _value, bytes _operatorData) external;
}
```

Let's explore the following functions provided in the interface:

- The following function returns all of the partitions associated with a token holder address:

  ```
  function partitionsOf(address _tokenHolder) external view returns
  (bytes32[]);
  ```

- This function passes bytes_data to be submitted when the transfer happens; the token contract can interpret or record the data and determine the receiver's partition:

  ```
  function transferByPartition(bytes32 _partition, address _to,
  uint256 _value, bytes _data) external returns (bytes32);
  ```

- This function allows an operator to transfer security tokens on behalf of a token holder, within a specified partition. It allows performing corporate actions, like mergers and acquisitions, which are essential for financial assets:

```
function operatorTransferByPartition(bytes32 _partition, address
_from, address _to, uint256 _value, bytes _data, bytes
_operatorData) external returns (bytes32);
```

The ERC-1400 security token standards represent a library of standards for security tokens. It contains the following list of EIP standards:

- **ERC-1410**: Differentiated ownership/transparent restrictions
- **ERC-1594**: On-chain and off-chain transfer restrictions and issuance/redemption semantics
- **ERC-1643**: Document/legend management
- **ERC-1644**: Controller operations (force transfer)

The ERC-1400 implements the partial fungibility property. This property allows performing corporate actions, such as document management, controller operations, mergers, and acquisitions, which are essential for financial assets.

The standard implements the following ERC-1400 interface:

```
/// @title IERC1400 Security Token Standard
interface IERC1400 is IERC20 {
    // Document Management
    function getDocument(bytes32 name) external view returns (string,
bytes32);
    function setDocument(bytes32 name, string uri, bytes32 documentHash)
external;
    event Document(bytes32 indexed name, string uri, bytes32 documentHash);

    // Controller Operation
    function isControllable() external view returns (bool);

    // Token Issuance
    function isIssuable() external view returns (bool);
    function issueByPartition(bytes32 partition, address tokenHolder,
uint256 value, bytes data) external;
    event IssuedByPartition(bytes32 indexed partition, address indexed
operator, address indexed to, uint256 value, bytes data, bytes
operatorData);

    // Token Redemption
    function redeemByPartition(bytes32 partition, uint256 value, bytes
data) external;
```

```
    function operatorRedeemByPartition(bytes32 partition, address
tokenHolder, uint256 value, bytes data, bytes operatorData) external;
    event RedeemedByPartition(bytes32 indexed partition, address indexed
operator, address indexed from, uint256 value, bytes data, bytes
operatorData);

    // Transfer Validity
    function canTransferByPartition(bytes32 partition, address to, uint256
value, bytes data) external view returns (byte, bytes32, bytes32);
    function canOperatorTransferByPartition(bytes32 partition, address
from, address to, uint256 value, bytes data, bytes operatorData) external
view returns (byte, bytes32, bytes32);

}
```

The `getDocument/setDocument` function provides document access that is associated with a token. The `isControllable` function checks whether the token can be controlled by operators. The `redeemByPartition` function ID is used to redeem tokens of a specific partition. The `canTransferByPartition` function is used to check if a token is allowed to be transferred by the partition.

Partial substitutability is a major component of the ERC-1400 pass standard, which means that one ERC-1400 pass issued by the same entity may not be exchanged with another ERC-1400 pass because the pass may have different attributes. The most popular irreplaceable pass is, of course, CryptoKitties based on the ERC-721 standard: you don't exchange a kitten directly, because each kitten is unique and the price varies. However, ERC-1400 passes are not necessarily different from each other like CryptoKitties, so they are partially interchangeable.

Another function of ERC-1400 interchangeability is to support the split and combination functions of the license.

ST-20 (security token standard)

The ST-20 token is an Ethereum-based token synonymous with ERC-1400/EC-1410. It was built at Polymath. Polymath is a security token issuance platform that uses the ST-20 token standard to connect between financial securities and the blockchain. It is a platform that is built on top of a decentralized protocol and manages the whole security token life cycle, including creating security tokens and conducting security token offerings to ensure regulatory compliance with securities laws.

ST-20 is an extension of ERC-20 and adds one key `verifyTransfer` method. This method must be called during token transfer. The method checks whether a transfer will succeed or fail. If it fails, it will output the reasons for failure.

Here is how the ST-20 interface looks:

```
contract IST20 {

    // represents off-chain hash
    bytes32 public tokenDetails;

    //transfer, transferFrom must respect the result of verifyTransfer
    function verifyTransfer(address _from, address _to, uint256 _amount)
view public returns (bool success);

    //used to create tokens
    function mint(address _investor, uint256 _amount) public returns (bool
success);
}
```

The implementation of `verifyTransfer` can vary. ST-20 tokens rely on transfer managers to control the whitelist. The default implementation for transfer managers is `GeneralTransferManager`. The mint function is used to create tokens.

The following diagram shows the Polymath network architecture:

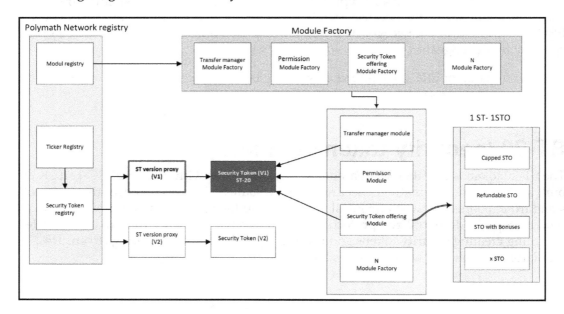

The following are a few core components in the network:

- Polymath registries
- **Module Factory**
- Module
- **ST version proxy**

Polymath registries have a **Ticker registry**, **Module registry**, and **Security Token registry**. A set of registries manages security tokens and their available modules. The token is unique in the polymath network. The **Ticker registry** maintains the unique token symbol *reservation* and makes sure that new symbol tokens are not duplicated in the network.

The **Security Token registry** keeps the version of **Security Token** issued on the Polymath platform. When a new version of **Security Token** is deployed to the network, the registry maintains a record for these tokens. It can then call the new version of **Security Token** via the **ST version proxy** mechanism.

The platform supports various modules: **Transfer manager module**, **Permission Module**, **Security Token offering Module**, and so on; each module serves a different purpose. By using the factory design pattern, these modules are generated from the related module factory. This pattern provides the flexibility to generate various modules that the business requires.

As we discussed before, the default implementation for transfer managers is `GeneralTransferManager`. This is provided by transfer modules. In transfer modules, the following two transfer modules were released in the Polymath platform:

- **Transfer manager module**: This is a general-approach whitelist-based transfer module. When a transfer is called, `transferFrom` and `verifyTransfer` will use this module to check if the addresses are mapped in the whitelist. It holds a list of verified investors and their sale/purchase restrictions.
- **Exchange transfer manager module**: This module handles dealing with centralized exchanges.

Permission modules give the issuer flexibility on account permission control and manages their whitelisting process.

The **Security Token offering module** controls a token's initial issuance/sale, like ICOs crowdsale contracts. For example, raise in POLY or ETH, start and end dates, hard cap, exchange rate, and so on.

R-Token

R-Token was developed by Harbor. It is built on ERC-20, and enforces regulatory compliance at the token level.

The R-Token includes the following three core components:

- The token itself
- The regulator service
- The service registry

These components are shown in the following diagram:

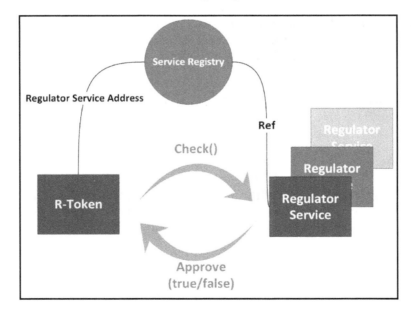

As a permission token, **R-Token** transfer is controlled by the on-chain regulator service. RegulatorService's `check()` method will be called within the `transfer()` and `transferFrom()` methods in the R-Token contract. The token can be transferred after the regular service completes the check and approval. If the check is unsuccessful, the error code returns. The error reason code is emitted on the event log. Here is the `check` method on `RegulatorService`:

```
contract RegulatorService {
    function check(address _token,
        address _spender,
        address _from,
        address _to,
        uint256 _amount) public returns (uint8);
    event RedeemedByPartition(bytes32 indexed partition, address indexed
    operator, address indexed
    }
```

The configuration in `RegulatorService` can be updated to meet any number of regulatory requirements, including KYC policies, AML requirements, securities, investor accreditation, and so on. The service registry registers the `RegulatorService` address and routes the R-Token to the correct version of `RegulatorService` by changing a `RegulatorService` address.

To control the token level and participant level permission, the permission needs to be updated by an off-chain trade controller. It checks the participant data against defined KYC/AML policies, securities regulations, and so on to determine the participant permission to receive or send the token and the partial trading permission. Only an approved trade controller can call the regulator service by the private/public key. The token level permission includes locked and partial amounts, which control the partial token amount.

Participant level permission includes PERM_SEND and PERM_RECV, which provide the permission to send and receive a token from another account.

The process is illustrated in the following diagram:

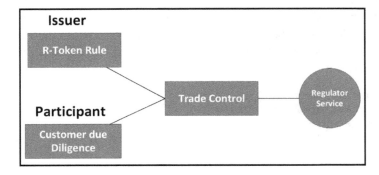

Let's now look at SRC-20.

SRC-20

SRC-20 is a standard ERC-20 token. The SRC-20 protocol standard is designed by Swarm Fund, a real-world asset tokenizing blockchain platform. SRC-20 security tokens are built on TokenD and the Stellar blockchain.

On the Swarm platform, real-world objects can be set as tokenized assets using the SRC-20 protocol. These objects include real estates, tech companies, hedge funds, and so on. These tokenized assets can be purchased, traded, or simply held. Rules are defined in the SRC-20 protocol to make sure SRC-20 tokens must follow to represent a real-world asset. Individuals can invest real-world assets by buying security tokens (SRC-20) on Swarm's private blockchain. Swarm's private blockchain has the ability to trade tokens in a regulatory-compliant manner. These SRC-20 tokens can also interoperate with other compliant platforms.

The Swarm ecosystem has the following two types of token:

- The Swarm token (SWM)
- The SRC-20 tokens

SWM is a utility token. Applications can communicate with each other by paying SWM for transactions, such as ether in Ethereum. The Swarm utility token has a limited supply of 100 M tokens. SRC-20 tokens represent ownership of that investment. Investment platforms, asset management suites, and so on can be built using the SRC-20 protocol.

The following diagram illustrates how a user can hold, invest, and refund through the SRC-20 protocol:

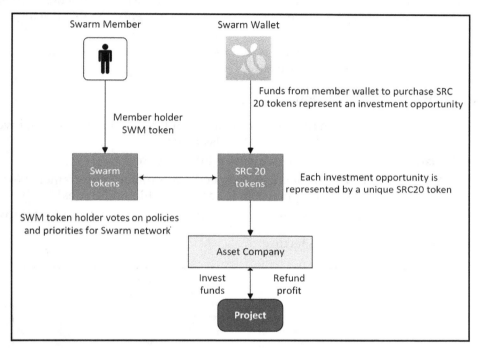

Let's now look at DS- Token.

DS-Token (Securitize)

DS-Token is an ERC-20 token based on the **digital securities** (**DS**) protocol. The DS-Token standard is developed by Securitize. The DS protocol provides a compliant integration solution and address to resolve the fundraising, automation, and liquidity needs of financial assets for the entire digital security life cycle; the protocol makes sure that compliance is achieved at the token level.

Securitize's digital ownership architecture

The DS architecture contains a set of components and services that allow third parties (developers) to enhance and extend the DS ecosystem, and governs DS service elements with the entire structure, allowing these interactions between DS apps and DS-Tokens.

Let's now look at **DS apps** and **DS service**:

- **DS apps**: DS protocol applications handle each stage of the functionality during the digital security life cycle, such as governance events, flexible pricing during investment flow, issuance, paying dividends, and voting rights
- **DS service**: The DS protocol service enables life cycle management and compliance for digital securities

These services will include the following:

- **Trust service**: For managing different stakeholders (issuer, exchanges, investor) and DS apps to be used for an existing issuance
- **Registration service**: On-chain investor information
- **Compliance services**: Implementing specific compliance requirements for DS-Tokens and applying compliance in token ownership and trades
- **Communication services**: Providing communication events to relevant investors

Here is an overview of the DS architecture:

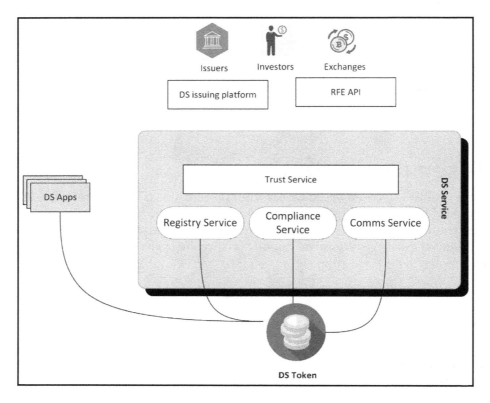

The DS protocol provides the DS-Token package to create useful ERC-20 tokens. DSTokenBase and DSToken are included in the package. You can extend from DSTokenBase for a standard ERC-20 with your business logic.

DSToken extends from the DSTokenBase interface; plus the DSAuth-protected mint and burns functions push, pull, and move are used for transferFrom operations.

The following are smart contract function implementations for DSToken:

```
contract DSToken is DSTokenBase(0), DSStop {
 ...
    function approve(address guy, uint wad) public stoppable returns (bool)
{
        return super.approve(guy, wad);
    }
    function transferFrom(address src, address dst, uint wad) public
        stoppable returns (bool) {
        if (src != msg.sender && _approvals[src][msg.sender] != uint(-1)) {
            require(_approvals[src][msg.sender] >= wad, "ds-token-
insufficient-approval");
            _approvals[src][msg.sender] = sub(_approvals[src][msg.sender],
wad);
        }
        require(_balances[src] >= wad, "ds-token-insufficient-balance");
        _balances[src] = sub(_balances[src], wad);
        _balances[dst] = add(_balances[dst], wad);
        emit Transfer(src, dst, wad);
        return true;
    }
    function push(address dst, uint wad) public {
        transferFrom(msg.sender, dst, wad);
    }
    function pull(address src, uint wad) public {
        transferFrom(src, msg.sender, wad);
    }
    function move(address src, address dst, uint wad) public {
        transferFrom(src, dst, wad);
    }
    function mint(address guy, uint wad) public auth stoppable {
        _balances[guy] = add(_balances[guy], wad);
        _supply = add(_supply, wad);
        emit Mint(guy, wad);
    }
    function burn(address guy, uint wad) public auth stoppable {
        if (guy != msg.sender && _approvals[guy][msg.sender] != uint(-1)) {
            require(_approvals[guy][msg.sender] >= wad, "ds-token-
insufficient-approval");
```

```
            _approvals[guy][msg.sender] = sub(_approvals[guy][msg.sender],
    wad);
        }

        require(_balances[guy] >= wad, "ds-token-insufficient-balance");
        _balances[guy] = sub(_balances[guy], wad);
        _supply = sub(_supply, wad);
        emit Burn(guy, wad);
    }
    ..
}
```

DSAuth makes sure that the function is only called by specifically authorized addresses as follows:

```
contract AppTokenController is DSAuth, DSMath {

    ERC20 deposit;
    DSToken appToken;
    SystemRules rules;
    function cashOut(uint128 wad) {
        assert(rules.canCashOut(msg.sender));
        uint prize = wdiv(wad, rules.serviceFee());
        appToken.pull(msg.sender, wad);
        // only this contract is authorized to burn tokens
        appToken.burn(prize);
        deposit.transfer(msg.sender, prize);
    }
    function newRules(SystemRules rules_) auth {
        rules = rules_;
    }
}
```

AppTokenController extends from DSAuth; the newRules function can update the existing rule under Auth permission. The rule will use the cashOut function to make sure the sender's address is authorized.

ERC-1404

The ERC-1404 token standard is proposed by Ron Gierlach (@rongierlach), James Poole (@pooleja), Mason Borda (@masonicGIT), and so on. It is an EIP subtype. The EIP title is a simple restricted token standard. The current EIP status is draft.

ERC-1404 is a self-regulatory token, a simple restricted token standard. It extends the ERC20 interface and adds some restrictions on a token to help enforce regulatory compliance as follows:

```
contract ERC20 {
    function totalSupply() public view returns (uint256);
    function balanceOf(address who) public view returns (uint256);
    function transfer(address to, uint256 value) public returns (bool);
    function allowance(address owner, address spender) public view returns
(uint256);
    function transferFrom(address from, address to, uint256 value) public
returns (bool);
    function approve(address spender, uint256 value) public returns (bool);
    event Approval(address indexed owner, address indexed spender, uint256
value);
    event Transfer(address indexed from, address indexed to, uint256 value);
}
```

ERC1404 adds two more functions by extending ERC20 to enforce transfer restrictions as follows:

```
contract ERC1404 is ERC20 {
    // return 0 - success
    function detectTransferRestriction (address from,
                        address to,
                        uint256 value
    ) public view returns (uint8);
    function messageForTransferRestriction (
                                uint8 restrictionCode
    ) public view returns (string);
}
```

The messageForTransferRestriction() function returns a human-readable message for a given restriction code that tells the user why a transaction is restricted.

detectTransferRestriction has the following functionality:

- It needs to be executed by the issuer
- If return is not equal to 0, the transaction needs to be reverted
- It must be executed within transfer()/transferFrom()

- The issuer needs to implement the following restrictions:
  - Check if the receiver is on a whitelist
  - Check if the sender's token is in the lockout period
  - The third party can also call the interface to learn if the transfer is restricted
  - If return is not equal to 0, the caller can know the cause of the failure and change the type of processing for various reasons

ERC-1404 provides several features as follows:

- Helps the token issuer create and maintain a whitelist of investor addresses that control who can own the token
- Able to set a limit for the amount of investment for individual investors across all crowdfunding offerings
- Allows human-readable messages to be implemented when the token is reverted
- Provides a tool to carry complex compliance requirements
- Allows building time limitation and other conditions into the token
- Supports other security token standards such as Polymath's ST-20 or Harbor's R-Token
- An easy GitHub example implementation

In the preceding ERC-1404 features, we can see that there are many restrictions added to the token (time limit, complex compliance requirements, a limit for the amount, and so on); therefore, the token issuer can control when those tokens can be transferred and the number of tokens that can be transferred. This allows tokens to be transferred only after the investor passes a KYC check. ERC-1404 can be designed for token lock-ups to protect the token value when developers and investors are not allowed to sell their token at an early stage.

ERC-884

The Delaware State Legislature passed Title 8 of the Delaware Code relating to the General Corporation Law on July 21, 2017. The law allows Delaware corporations to use blockchain technologies to create a tradable ERC-20 token and maintain shares issued by a Delaware corporation. ERC-884 is designed to comply with Delaware General Corporate Law. The token is an ERC-20 compatible token, and David Sag developed the token standard.

In an ERC-884 token, token owners must verify their identity. Whitelist shareholders can issue tokens. The whitelist rules are defined in Sections 219 and 220 of the act. The blockchain needs records of the information, which is specified in sections 156, 159, 217(a), and 218 of the act. While transferring the token, the smart contract function needs to comply with Article 8 of Subtitle I of Title 6. It doesn't allow partial token transfer. The shareholder name and address need to be kept up to date; this will implement off-chain private data to store the owner's information. The updateVerified functions in the contract are designed for this purpose. They will compare the hash on-chain and off-chain. When the hash matches, the function can read private shareholder information from off-chain data. In ERC-884, the cancelAndReissue method can cancel the shareholder address and reissue the token to the new address when a token owner loses their private key or loses access to their token.

The ERC-884 token provides the following basic features. Here is the Solidity code:

```solidity
contract ERC884 is ERC20 {
    event VerifiedAddressAdded(
        address indexed addr,
        bytes32 hash,
        address indexed sender
    );
    event VerifiedAddressRemoved(
        address indexed addr,
        address indexed sender
    );
    event VerifiedAddressUpdated(
        address indexed addr,
        bytes32 oldHash,
        bytes32 hash,
        address indexed sender
    );
    event VerifiedAddressSuperseded(
        address indexed original,
        address indexed replacement,
        address indexed sender
    );
    function addVerified(address addr, bytes32 hash) public;
    function removeVerified(address addr) public;
    function updateVerified(address addr, bytes32 hash) public;
    function cancelAndReissue(
        address original,
        address replacement
    ) public;
    function transfer(
        address to,
        uint256 value
```

```
) public returns (bool);
function transferFrom(
    address from,
    address to,
    uint256 value
 ) public returns (bool);
function isVerified(address addr) public view returns (bool);
function isHolder(address addr) public view returns (bool);
function hasHash(
    address addr,
    bytes32 hash
) public view returns (bool);
function holderCount() public view returns (uint);
function holderAt(uint256 index) public view returns (address);
function isSuperseded(address addr) public view returns (bool);
function getCurrentFor(
    address addr
) public view returns (address);
}
```

Here is a summary of the functions:

- addVerified: Add a verified address along with an associated hash to blockchain
- removeVerified: Remove a verified address and associated hash by a given address
- updateVerified: Update the hash for a given verified address
- cancelAndReissue: Cancel the shareholder address and reissue the token to the new address
- isVerified: Verify if the input address is valid
- isHolder: Check the given address holds a token
- hasHash: Check the given hash associated with the token address
- holderCount: Get the total number of tokens for the given address
- holderAt: Get the complete list of token holders information by entering index number
- isSuperseded: Check the address is superseded
- getCurrentFor: Is given a superseded address and returns the most recent address

We just overviewed popular security token standards in the current blockchain space. There are many other security token standards; here are a few of them:

- **OpenFinance Network: Smart Securities Standard (S3)**. It has three modules:
    - The interface
    - The compliance layer
    - The data layer

    S3 allows tokens to be traded between buyers and sellers only when regulation and compliance requirements are met.

- **ERC-1450**: ERC-1450 is an ERC-20-compatible token. The standard was proposed by John Shiple, Howard Marks, and David Zhang. ERC-1450 manages securities ownership and trades securities in compliance with Securities Act Regulations CF, D, and A. Only the contract issuer can create an ERC-1450 token and assign the **registered transfer agent** (**RTA**). Only RTA is allowed to execute ERC-1450's `mint()`, `burnFrom()`, and an SEC-registered broker-dealer completes the `transferFrom` functions after a trade.

In the next section, we will quickly review the smart contract Solidity programming language; if you already know this topic, you can skip this section and proceed to the next chapter. In the next chapter, we will run some smart contracts and build a simple app for security tokens.

Introduction to smart contracts

Nick Szabo introduced the smart contract concept in 1994. A smart contract is specific executable computer logic and code built within a peer-to-peer blockchain network. When a certain condition is met, the smart contract will automatically execute a contract instruction and update the ledger in the blockchain. Each smart contract is assigned a unique address in the blockchain. When the smart contract executes, it is run by each node as part of block creation.

In the Ethereum blockchain, the programming language for the smart contract is Solidity. It was developed by Gavin Wood, Christian Reitwiessner, and several Ethereum core contributors. Solidity is a statically-typed language, similar to JavaScript and C. When Solidity is compiled, it checks the variable type and turns it into Ethereum virtual machine byte code; once it deploys to the Ethereum network, it will be assigned a contact address. Several other programming languages can write a smart contract as well; the most popular contract language in Ethereum is Solidity.

In this section, we will have a quick overview of the key concepts of the Solidity programming language, and in Chapter 6, *Building a Security Token Dapp*, we will develop some very basic security token smart contracts.

Let's explore the most basic smart contract example, HelloWorld.sol, as follows:

```
pragma solidity ^0.5.4;
// Hello World single-line comment.
contract HelloWorld {

    uint myData;
    /** @dev set myData value.
     *   @param x input data.
     */
     function set(uint x) public {
         myData = x;
     }
    /**@dev get myData value.
     *   @return output mydata.
     */
     function get() public view returns (uint) {
         return myData;
     }
}
```

In the HelloWorld example, Solidity's file extension is .sol. It is similar to .js for JavaScript files and .html for HTML templates.

The example file also includes many basic Solidity syntaxes.

Pragma

The first line, which contains the Pragma keyword indicates that the source code file is not intended to be compiled by Solidity compiler earlier than version 0.5.4. Anything newer does not break the functionality. The ^ symbol implies another condition—the source file will also not work on compilers later than version 0.5.4.

Comments

Comments are a human-readable description to remind the coder (and inform others about the functions of the program. They are used to make it easier for humans to understand the source code and function of the program. Comments are ignored by the Solidity compiler. Two forms of comment are supported in Solidity: single-line comments, starting with `//`, and other is multi-line comments (used for large text descriptions of code). Multi-line comments start with `/*` and end with `*/`.

In the `Helloworld` example, there are multi-line comments for the `set` and `get` methods as follows:

- **Method 1**:

    ```
    function set(uint x) public {}
    ```

    `@param`: This is used to indicate what parameters are being passed to a method, and what value they're expected to have

- **Method 2**:

    ```
    function get() public view returns (uint) {}
    ```

    `@return`: This is used to indicate what result the method is going to give back

Import

The `import` keyword in Solidity is very similar to JavaScript's past version ES6 import syntax. It is used to import libraries and other related features into your Solidity source file. Solidity does not support export statements.

Here are a few import examples:

```
import {symbol1 as alias, symbol2} from "soldityfile"
```

The preceding line will create two global symbols called alias and `symbol2`, containing the global symbol members from the import file `solidityfile`.

Here is an example to calculate `mul256By256` using Solidity arithmetic libraries; the function multiplies two unsigned 256-bit integers and returns a 512-bit result:

```
import "./path/to/Arithmetic.sol";

contract MyContract {
    function myFunction() {
        uint x, y;
        // handle Arithmetic function use import library
        uint result = Arithmetic.mul256By256(x, y);
    }
}
```

For example, we imported the `Arithmetic.sol` and applied it to `myFunction` in `MyContract`.

Paths

When importing a Solidity file, the file path follows the following simple syntax rules:

- **Absolute paths**:

  ```
  import "filename";
  ```

  When the filename does not start with `.`, it considers it as an absolute path and treats it as a path with `/` as the directory separator.

- **Relative paths**:

  ```
  '../folder1/folder2/xxx.sol':
  ```

  These paths are interpreted relative to the location of the current file; `.` means the current directory and `..` means the parent directory.

In the Solidity path, you can specify path prefix remappings. As an example, if you want to import `github.com/libs/bin`, you can first clone the GitHub library to `local/usr/local/bin/lib`, and then run the following compiler command:

```
solc github.com/libs/bin=/usr/local/bin/lib
```

Then, in our Solidity file, you can use the following `import` statement. It will remap to `/usr/local/dapp-bin/library/stringUtils.sol`:

```
import "github.com/ethereum/dapp-bin/library/stringUtils.sol " as
stringUtils;
```

The compiler will read the files from there.

State variables

State variables are referred to as values that maintain the contract's state. They are permanently stored in contract storage.

Here is an example:

```
contract SimpleStorage {
    uint storedData; // State variable
    //...
}
```

Functions

Functions defined in a contract are executable units. Here is the function structure in Solidity:

```
function (<Input parameters>) {access modifiers}
[pure|constant|view|payable] [returns (<return types>)]
```

Let's look at the code, as follows:

```
pragma solidity >=0.4.0 <0.6.0;

contract MyAuction {
    function add(uint _x, uint _y) public pure returns (uint o_sum) {
        o_sum = _x + _y;
    }}
```

The Solidity function can return types with multiple values, for example, return (v0, v1, ..., vn). You can directly return a value with the return statement or explicitly return variable and leave the function using return as follows:

```
contract MyAuction {
    function add(uint _x, uint _y) public pure returns (uint o_sum) {
        return (_x + _y);
    }}
```

When the function is declared as view, the function will not modify the storage state.

Pure is more restrictive when the function is declared as `pure`; it means that the function won't even read the storage state.

Function modifiers

In Solidity, `modifier` is used to add some modification or extra checks to a function. `modifier` will validate to make sure all conditions are met before executing the function.

Here is an example to show how a crowdfunding smart contract can use a modifier to add a constraint on the `checkGoalReached` function. In this function, it only allows the contract owner to check if the crowdfunding goal is reached after the project passes the deadline:

```
contract CrowdFunding {
..
//check if msg.sender is project owner
modifier onlyOwner() {
    require(project.addr == msg.sender,"Only Owner Allowed." );
    _;
}
//check if project pass the deadline
modifier afterDeadline() {
    require(now >= project.deadline);
    _;
}
function checkGoalReached() public onlyOwner afterDeadline {
  ....
}
}
```

In the preceding example, `checkGoalReached` is only executed by the owner after the project deadline has passed.

Events

Events are used to track the execution of a transaction sent to a contract; there are convenient interfaces with **Ethereum virtual machine** (**EVM**) logging facilities.

In the `Crowdfunding` contract example, we define the `LogFundingReceived` event to received fund amount transaction as follows:

```
contract CrowdFunding {
..
event LogFundingReceived(address addr, uint amount, uint currentTotal);
function fund() public atStage(Status.Fundraising) payable
{contributions.push(
Contribution({
addr: msg.sender,
amount: msg.value
})
);
project.totalRaised += msg.value;
project.currentBalance = project.totalRaised;
emit LogFundingReceived(msg.sender, msg.value, project.totalRaised);
}
}
```

To trigger an `event`, Solidity uses the `emit` keyword followed by the event name with an argument for the `event` function. It can be used by UI JavaScript callbacks, which listen for these events.

struct

A `struct` is a type that contains user-defined custom fields. New types can be declared using a `struct`. The following is an example:

```
struct address {
        string name;
        string city;
        string state;
        string country;
    }
```

enum

enum is a type defining a restricted set of constant values. The following is an example:

```
contract MyContract {
    enum Day {
      SUNDAY, MONDAY, TUESDAY, WEDNESDAY, THURSDAY, FRIDAY, SATURDAY
    }
}
```

Inheritance, abstract, and interface

Many of the most widely used programming languages (such as C++, Java, Go, Python, and so on) support **object-oriented programming (OOP)** and support inheritance, encapsulation, abstraction, and polymorphism. Inheritance enables code reuse and extensibility. Solidity supports multiple inheritances in the form of copying code, which includes polymorphism. Like many other programming languages, even if a contract inherits multiple other contracts, nevertheless only a single contract is created by the compiler and deployed to the blockchain.

In Solidity, inheritance is pretty similar to classic oriented-object programming languages. The following is an example:

```
pragma solidity ^0.5.0;
interface Token {
    enum TokenType { Fungible, NonFungible }
    struct Coin { string name; }
    function totalSupply() view external returns (uint);
    function balanceOf(address tokenOwner) view external returns (uint
balance);
}
contract AbstractTokenBase is Token {
    mapping(address => uint256) balances;
    TokenType ttype;
    function balanceOf(address tokenOwner) public view returns (uint
balance) {
        return balances[tokenOwner];
    }
}
contract AToken is AbstractTokenBase {
    function totalSupply() public view returns (uint) {
        return 1000;
    }
        function getTokenType() public pure returns (TokenType){
        return TokenType.NonFungible;
    }
}
contract BToken is AbstractTokenBase {
    function totalSupply() public view returns (uint) {
        return 3000;
    }
    function getTokenType() public pure returns (TokenType){
        return TokenType.Fungible;
    }
}
```

In Solidity, a method without a body (no implementation) is known as an abstract method. A contract that contains an abstract method cannot be instantiated but can be used as a base contract.

If a contract extends from an abstract contract, then the contract must implement all the abstract methods of the abstract parent class, or it has to declare an abstract as well.

Interfaces in Solidity are similar to abstract contracts; they are implicitly abstract and cannot have implementations. An abstract contract can have instance methods that implement a default behavior.

There are the following restrictions in an interface:

- It does not allow you to inherit other contracts or interfaces
- It does not allow you to define a constructor
- It does not allow you to define variables
- It does not allow you to define structs

`AbstractTokenBase` inherits from `Token`; the interface defines the `enum` token type, `Coin` struct, `totalSupply`, and `balanceOf` functions. `AbstractTokenBase` has one concrete function `balanceOf`, and the unimplemented `totalSupply` function. Therefore `AbstractTokenBase` is an abstract contract.

`AToken` and `BToken` extend from `AbstractTokenBase`, and implement the `totalSupply`, `AToken`, and `BToken` inheritance interface `Token` and the `AbstractTokenBase` abstract class.

`getTokenType()` in `AToken` and `BToken` can read the `enum` token type value defined in the `Token` interface.

Summary

In this chapter, we covered the following popular security token standards: ERC-1400/ERC-1410, R-Token, DS-Token, SRC-20, ST-20, S3, ERC-884, ERC-1450, and ERC-1404. Although we only talk about the security token fundamental, I hope it can help you to enrich your knowledge of security token protocols. We have learned the basics of Solidity programming and we understood the basic syntax of smart contracts.

In the next chapter, we will continue our learning journey: we'll start to build a security token Dapp and write a smart contract based on one of the security token protocols we've discussed.

Building a Security Token Dapp

6

In the previous chapter, Chapter 5, *Security Token Smart Contracts*, we learned about the popular security token standards and an overview of the basic Solidity smart contract language. We should be quite comfortable with the fundamentals of the security token smart contract. In this chapter, we are going to write a security token smart contract and build a Dapp. We will be utilizing the **Truffle** development tool to help develop, test, debug, and deploy our security token Dapp.

This chapter is organized around five major topics, as follows:

- **Security token offerings** (**STO**) smart contract development tools
- Setting up an Ethereum development environment
- Creating a security token Truffle project
- Developing and testing a security token smart contract
- Writing Dapp web components

STO smart contract development tools

There are many popular smart contract tools available; in our STO sample contract, we chose Truffle and Ganache as our development environment tools. Truffle is one of the most popular Solidity Dapp development tools. Ganache provides you with a private Ethereum blockchain environment locally, which is very easy to set up.

Truffle

Truffle is a popular Ethereum development tool that provides a development environment, testing framework, and much other easy-to-use toolsets to make Ethereum development easier. With Truffle, you can have a compiled smart contract and automated smart contract testing with **Mocha** and **Chai**. The configuration supports deploying contracts to the local and public network.

You can write HTML, CSS, and JavaScript for the frontend; the web UI uses the web3.js API to interact with the smart contract in the Ethereum blockchain. **Truffle Boxes** provide helpful boilerplates, which contain useful configuration, JavaScript, Solidity contracts, libraries, and many other helpful files. The boxes help developers quickly set up and get started with their Dapp project.

The `truffle` command line uses the following format:

```
truffle [command] [options]
```

Here are the most frequently used options in command-line tools:

Command	Description
compile	Compile Solidity contract files
console	Command-line interface to interact with deployed smart contract
create	This command helps to create a new contract, new migration file, and a basic test
test	Run solidity smart contract tests
deploy/migration	Deploy contract to blockchain network
develop	Interact with a contract via the command line in a local development environment
init	Install a package from the Ethereum package registry

Ganache

Ganache is a private Ethereum blockchain environment that emulates the Ethereum network so that you can deploy and interact with smart contracts in your private blockchain. Here are some features that Ganache provides:

- Displays blockchain log output
- Provides advanced mining control

- Built-in block explorer
- Ethereum blockchain environment
- Comes with a desktop application, as well as a command-line tool

Here is what the desktop version of Ganache looks like:

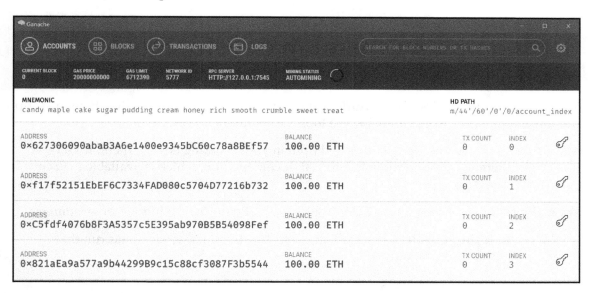

The command line uses the following format:

```
ganache-cli <options>
```

Here are some frequently used options in command-line tools:

Options	Description
-a or --accounts	How many accounts to generate at startup.
-e or --defaultBalanceEther	Configures the default test account ether amount; the default is 100.
-b or --blockTime	Specifies the block time in seconds as the mining interval. If this option is not specified, Ganache will instantly mine a new block when a transaction is invoked.
-h or --host or --hostname	Specifies the hostname to listen on; the default is 127.0.0.1.
-p or --port	Specifies the port number; the default is 8545.

-g or --gasPrice	Specifies the gas price in Wei (defaults to 20000000000).
-l or --gasLimit	The block gas limit (defaults to 0x6691b7).
--debug	Displays VM opcodes for debugging purposes.
-q or --quiet	Runs ganache-cli without any logs.

Setting up an Ethereum development environment

We just learned the basics of the Truffle and Ganache development tools. It is time to set up our development environment using the tools we mentioned previously.

Make sure you have installed Node.js and npm in your working environment. If you haven't set them up, please follow the official documentation, which is available at https://www.npmjs.com/get-npm.

We will install the following tools. This book's example runs in a Windows environment:

- **Installing Truffle**: Open the command-line terminal window and run the following command:

```
npm install -g truffle@4.1.12
```

- **Installing Ganache**: Open the command-line terminal and install Ganache's command-line interface:

```
npm install -g ganache-cli
```

- **Launching Ganache environment**: Once Ganache is installed, verify and start Ganache by running the following command:

```
ganache-cli
```

You should see something like this in your console:

```
Ganache CLI v6.1.0 (ganache-core: 2.1.0)

Available Accounts
==================
(0) 0xef18baedab2a76cf9e564f2f7cc32ef5d976207d
(1) 0x5b4c84cf76fc917970a5f98e825ebeb700ff208c
(2) 0xe01c417a907dd8e8dfb405211f72ca50b59a93ea
(3) 0x892a0ec934a4aba520dafa88f1d792260f553fd5
(4) 0x73d6abafacafc414bb8b63788fa3f5175f89cce3
(5) 0xaf4431b298333ec76f59c0ff5f231c6b1eb40449
(6) 0x1f06727631762824602ba60a13e9bc8ac6c78e3f
(7) 0x0954345c888733db4d8ef7dcd2e84135f8bf6f96
(8) 0x527c4367249f8bf28ef2eb859555fdebe22b7eb2
(9) 0x2933810a066c8cf890b583ecbc708852dae748f0

Private Keys
==================
(0) a02d2bb754a555266379768b5ba54aac1e259078e5b43cb0ef3ec3d8dcf1b188
(1) aeae9066fb87841398714b00bf9edc9cf2b297788ff00eaf0294759d6ea7a5cd
(2) 81b5451551bbf376abcd14be49bec8c7e4094a34db0e289deefa5648e45b82f0
(3) ce8124e5e3c69f4ae73d5a22cd30111256d57a3732246ba7a1b4bf2705e7f1dd
(4) 51282343720b7786103b6b134ddcca55e409a257806ccf2764293a0a6476f769
(5) d564efd8213822a4e4c5588b3e6ab734604043c0ce3a605ae979328239e0d5a3
(6) f55d530a63b4978f67dc6a6cc1da522f5f843f19e72fe32974027aafb1fba48b
(7) 77e09b035bef9cacb099b030da8dafe59b4271e2aa04b59614148d1bc450a09a
(8) 687d16661832f3d15656c35fcf6dab268ec78596d7c71c79219d45b395c98598
(9) 425197ea31567b7d4942b31f80d413ea7bcc2286ddd487ceea60ee4bd259222e

HD Wallet
==================
Mnemonic:      hurt vapor history diamond next meat seven dress hill fish inflict try
Base HD Path:  m/44'/60'/0'/0/{account_index}

Listening on localhost:8545
```

This will run `ganache-cli` on `8545` port; Ganache will create 10 default accounts for us. Each account will have 100 ether by default.

Creating a security token Truffle project

In this chapter, we will build ERC-1404—a **Simple Restricted Token Standard (SRTS)**. We will utilize extendable standard code provided by `https://erc1404.org/` to start our security token development based on the ERC-1404 standard. Here are the steps to start our security token development:

1. Run the following command to download the project template:

   ```
   git clone
   https://github.com/PacktPublishing/Security-Tokens-and-Stablecoins-
   Quick-Start-Guide.git
   ```

2. Navigate to the `simple-restricted-token` project folder; you should see the following prebuild project structure:

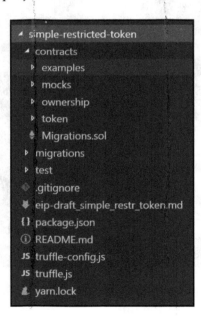

3. Install node libraries on the project root folder:

   ```
   npm install
   ```

   This will install project node dependencies.

4. Update the `truffle.js` file configuration.

    Since our Ganache runs on port `8545`, we need to update the `truffle.js` file configuration to connect to the Ganache server.

    Open `truffle.js`, and add the following network information. This will connect your simple security token Truffle project to your local Ganache server:

    ```
    module.exports = {
      networks: {
        development: {
          host: "127.0.0.1",
          port: 8545,
          network_id: "*" // Match any network id
        }
      }
    };
    ```

5. Compile the security token smart contract:

    `truffle compile`

This will compile all contracts from the `simple-restricted-token` project. You may see a warning message for a smart contract; we can ignore these messages:

```
Compiling .\contracts\Migrations.sol...
Compiling .\contracts\examples\divisibility\IndivisibleToken.sol...
Compiling .\contracts\examples\number-of-accounts\MaxNumShareholdersToken.sol...
Compiling .\contracts\examples\other-standards\R-Token\RegulatedTokenExample.sol...
Compiling .\contracts\examples\other-standards\R-Token\RegulatorServiceExample.sol...
Compiling .\contracts\examples\other-standards\ST20\ST20Example.sol...
Compiling .\contracts\examples\ownership-percentage\IndividualOwnershipStakeToken.sol...
Compiling .\contracts\examples\ownership-percentage\MaxOwnershipStakeToken.sol...
Compiling .\contracts\examples\whitelists\BasicWhitelistToken.sol...
Compiling .\contracts\examples\whitelists\ManagedWhitelist.sol...
Compiling .\contracts\examples\whitelists\ManagedWhitelistToken.sol...
Compiling .\contracts\mocks\BasicTokenMock.sol...
Compiling .\contracts\mocks\BasicWhitelistTokenMock.sol...
Compiling .\contracts\mocks\IndividualOwnershipStakeTokenMock.sol...
```

Let's learn to deploy security tokens to Ganache.

Deploying security tokens to Ganache

Truffle defines all smart contract deployment artifacts under `migrations/2_deploy_contracts.js`. The `simple-restricted-token` project has predefined lists of test contracts here; we can deploy and test these sample use cases directly.

Run the `truffle migrate` command to deploy mock contracts to Ganache:

```
truffle migrate
```

Here is the result after deploying smart contracts to the network:

```
Using network 'development'.

Running migration: 1_initial_migration.js
  Deploying Migrations...
  ... 0xc50c165b7645a9238ba7e66fc2726ab294fc5bcc1a9058981846144626bb1439
  Migrations: 0x3dc618e25d7d6469561743ee276aef4147724fda
Saving successful migration to network...
  ... 0x419f2d268233c539808cd131770e9c4c674d46336a03586362f4edee8ff731cc
Saving artifacts...
Running migration: 2_deploy_contracts.js
  Running step...
  Deploying MessagesAndCodes...
  ... 0x09b07834fd3261263a76829db20e74ff2cf03e00179f87e863f365ee33d62def
  MessagesAndCodes: 0x539be5b782074161969e0b152efa2754e8d5839e
  Linking MessagesAndCodes to IndivisibleTokenMock
  Linking MessagesAndCodes to BasicWhitelistTokenMock
  Linking MessagesAndCodes to ManagedWhitelistTokenMock
  Linking MessagesAndCodes to MaxOwnershipStakeTokenMock
  Linking MessagesAndCodes to MaxNumShareholdersTokenMock
  Linking MessagesAndCodes to IndividualOwnershipStakeTokenMock
  Linking MessagesAndCodes to ST20ExampleMock
Saving successful migration to network...
  ... 0xbebdf0428fc96e996b5e0098f8d30ea7357b4e6bd95d1e67359c6240b4d74edc
Saving artifacts...
```

You may notice that the Ganache console shows related transaction information; this verified that the smart contract had been deployed to the local blockchain network:

```
net_version
eth_sendTransaction

   Transaction: 0xc50c165b7645a9238ba7e66fc2726ab294fc5bcc1a9058981846144626bb1439
   Contract created: 0x3dc618e25d7d6469561743ee276aef4147724fda
   Gas usage: 277462
   Block Number: 1
   Block Time: Fri Mar 08 2019 17:51:01 GMT-0500 (Eastern Standard Time)

eth_newBlockFilter
eth_getFilterChanges
```

Now, we can run all these predefined `simple-restricted-token` test cases.

Type `truffle test` in the terminal under the project folder; this runs all test cases. If all goes well, you should see that all the test cases passed:

```
Contract: ST20Example
  √ should mint total supply of tokens to initial account
  √ should allow transfer between non-zero addresses (115ms)
  √ should allow transferFrom between non-zero addresses (after approval) (142ms)
  √ should deny transfer to the zero address
  √ should deny transferFrom to the zero address (after approval) (98ms)
  √ should detect success for transfer between non-zero addresses
  √ should detect zero address restriction for transfer to zero-address
  √ should return false for verifyTransfer call on transfer between non-zero addresses
  √ should return true for verifyTransfer call on transfer to zero-address
  √ should ensure success code is 0
  √ should return success message for success code
  √ should return restriction message for zero address restriction code
  √ should have tokenDetails set in the constructor
  √ should allow owner to mint tokens to an address (88ms)

Contract: RegulatedTokenExample
  √ should mint total supply of tokens to initial account
  √ should handle CHECK_ESEND condition (202ms)
  √ should handle CHECK_ERECV condition (248ms)
  √ should handle CHECK_ECDIVIS condition (259ms)
  √ should allow for valid transfer (248ms)
  √ should handle CHECK_ELOCKED condition (258ms)


87 passing (16s)
```

We have set up our development environment and project structure for our ERC-1404 token development. In the next section, we will define our token based on the standard library provided by the `simple-restricted-token` project.

Developing and testing a security token smart contract

As we discussed in the previous section, the ERC-1404 standard adds two more functions by extending ERC20 to enforce transfer restrictions—detectTransferRestriction and messageForTransferRestriction:

- messageForTransferRestriction returns a human-readable message for a given restriction code. The user can know why a transaction is restricted.
- The detectTransferRestriction function returns a non-zero value if the receiver address is not in the whiteList addresses, and the transaction needs to be reverted. The function needs to be executed by the token issuer.

Next, let's start to write our token and implement these functions.

 Other important ERC-1404 functions are adding an address to a whitelist, verifying a whitelist, and so on.

Creating a smart contract

Let's create a custom security ERC-1404 token smart contract under simple-restricted-token\contracts\token\ERC1404: MyERC1404.sol.

The smart contract we just created will extend from ERC1404, StandardToken, and Whitelist.

MyERC1404 will need to implement the detectTransferRestriction and messageForTransferRestriction methods that are defined in the ERC1404 interface.

We also need to utilize the Whitelist smart contract functions provided by the zeppelin-solidity library to manage Whitelist:

- addAddressToWhitelist(address _operator) adds an address to the whitelist function
- whitelist(address _operator) verifies whether the address is in the whitelist

Since the ERC1404 token extends from the ERC20 token, in MyERC1404, we extend the zeppelin-solidity library's StandardToken implementation, which provides the implementation of the basic standard token.

 In addition to the preceding features, we also provide some basic token information in MyERC1404, for example, name, symbol, and so on.

Implementing a smart contract

We will start by defining our token information first.

Defining your token information

We have learned from Chapter 5, *Security Token Smart Contracts*, that Solidity structures, such as a JavaScript object, define custom contract properties.

We will put all our token information in the TokenInfo structure. Moreover, when we deploy and instantiate our contract, we will enter a related token value to initialize this token information, as follows:

```
contract MyERC1404 is ERC1404, StandardToken, Whitelist {
    TokenInfo public tokenInfo;
    struct TokenInfo {
        address initialAccount;
        string name;
        string symbol;
        uint totalSupply;
    }
    constructor(string _name, string _symbol,  address initialAccount,
uint256 initialBalance) public{
        balances[initialAccount] = initialBalance;
        totalSupply_ = initialBalance;
        addAddressToWhitelist(initialAccount);
        tokenInfo = TokenInfo(initialAccount, _name,
_symbol,initialBalance);
    }
}
```

In our constructor, we will also add token issuer to the Whitelist address. The addAddressToWhitelist function is implemented by the zeppelin-solidity Whitelist smart contract.

Implementing detectTransferRestriction

We just defined our token information; now, we will implement the `detectTransferRestriction` method.

In `detectTransferRestriction`, we get a 0 return code as a restriction code for success. We can define `NON_WHITELIST_CODE` as 2. We also define the associate human-readable message for `SUCCESS` and the `NON_WHITELIST_CODE`, which can be used for `messageForTransferRestriction`.

Here is our definition of codes and messages:

```
uint8 public constant SUCCESS_CODE = 0;
string public constant SUCCESS_MESSAGE = "SUCCESS";
uint8 public constant NON_WHITELIST_CODE = 2;
string public constant NON_WHITELIST_ERROR =
"ILLEGAL_TRANSFER_TO_NON_WHITELISTED_ADDRESS";
```

You can define more return code and messages based on your token requirement.

`detectTransferRestriction` can be used to detect whether a transfer is in the approved `Whitelist`. When a transfer is not in the `Whitelist`, the transaction will be reverted.

Our contract extends the `zeppelin-solidity` `Whitelist` smart contract that has a `Whitelist (address _operator)` to check whether the address is in the `Whitelist`. We will use this method to check the receiving address in the `Whitelist` address to make the transfer. Otherwise, the method will return the `NON_WHITELIST_CODE`.

Here is the code logic:

```
function detectTransferRestriction (address from, address to, uint256
value)
    public
    view
    returns (uint8 restrictionCode)
{
    if (!whitelist(to)) {
        restrictionCode = NON_WHITELIST_CODE; // not allow for transfer
    } else {
        restrictionCode = SUCCESS_CODE; // in whitelist and successful
transfer
    }
}
```

Implementing messageForTransferRestriction

When we call the messageForTransferRestriction function with the restrictionCode input, it turns a related human-readable message. When the input is SUCCESS_CODE, the function will return SUCCESS_MESSAGE; if the input is NON_WHITELIST_CODE, it will return a NON_WHITELIST_ERROR message.

Here is the implementation:

```
function messageForTransferRestriction (uint8 restrictionCode)
    public
    view
    returns (string message)
{
    if (restrictionCode == SUCCESS_CODE) {
       message = SUCCESS_MESSAGE;
    } else if(restrictionCode == NON_WHITELIST_CODE) {
       message = NON_WHITELIST_ERROR;
    }
}
```

Implementing transfer and transferFrom

With the detectTransferRestriction and messageForTransferRestriction methods defined, we can apply these two restrict methods as a modifier to each token transfer. The modifier will check whether the recipient is in the Whitelist, and when detectTransferRestriction returns SUCCESS_CODE, the transfer can be executed in the blockchain. By applying a modifier, it will enforce certain restrictions for regulatory compliance, and the caller can find out about the cause of the failure if the transfer failed.

The following are the transfer and transferFrom methods' implementation logic:

```
modifier notRestricted (address from, address to, uint256 value) {
    uint8 restrictionCode = detectTransferRestriction(from, to, value);
    require(restrictionCode == SUCCESS_CODE,
 messageForTransferRestriction(restrictionCode));
    _;
}
    function transfer (address to, uint256 value)
        public
        notRestricted(msg.sender, to, value)
        returns (bool success)
    {
```

```
        success = super.transfer(to, value);
    }
    function transferFrom (address from, address to, uint256 value)
        notRestricted(from, to, value)
        returns (bool success)
    {
        success = super.transferFrom(from, to, value);
    }
```

In this step, we implemented our very simple ERC1404 token. Now, let's do some testing.

Testing a smart contract

In this section, we will implement unit test functions to test a smart contract. First, we will create a MyERC1404.js test class in the simple-restricted-token\test\token\ERC1404 folder.

Setting up and initializing the test case

First, we define and set up our test data before testing the ERC1404 main functions. This includes instantiating our contract with basic token information:

```
const MyERC1404 = artifacts.require('./token/ERC1404/MyERC1404')
contract('MyERC1404', ([owner, operator, ...accounts]) => {
  const initialAccount = owner
  const transferValue = '100000000000000000'
  const initialBalance = '100000000000000000000'
  const name ='MY1404Token'
  const symbol='MY1404'
  let token
  let tokenTotalSupply
  let SUCCESS_CODE
  let SUCCESS_MESSAGE
  let NON_WHITELIST_CODE
  let NON_WHITELIST_ERROR
  let sender = owner
  let recipient = operator
  before(async () => {
    token = await MyERC1404.new(name, symbol, initialAccount,
initialBalance)
    tokenTotalSupply = await token.totalSupply()
    SUCCESS_CODE = await token.SUCCESS_CODE()
    SUCCESS_MESSAGE = await token.SUCCESS_MESSAGE()
    NON_WHITELIST_CODE = await token.NON_WHITELIST_CODE()
```

```
    NON_WHITELIST_ERROR = await token.NON_WHITELIST_ERROR()
  })
}
```

First, we import the `MyERC1404` smart contract. In the Ganache 10 default accounts, we assign the first account as the `owner` account and the second account as the `operator` account. The `initialAccount` is the same as the owner account, which is the token issuer.

For our test case, we set `initialBalance` as 1 ether, which equals `100000000000000000` Wei. The transfer amount is set to 1 ether too. The token name is `MyERC1404` and the symbol is `My1404`.

In the `before()` test method, we instantiate the `MyERC1404` smart contract. Then, we assign `totalSupply`, `SUCCESS_CODE`, `NON_WHITELIST_CODE`, and `NON_WHITELIST_ERROR` to a local variable.

The `MyERC1404` contract extends the standard contract, and the `balanceOf` method can find sender and recipient balance information, as follows:

```
let senderBalanceBefore
let recipientBalanceBefore
beforeEach(async () => {
  senderBalanceBefore = await token.balanceOf(sender)
  recipientBalanceBefore = await token.balanceOf(recipient)
})
```

With all the test data set up, we can start to test our contract. First, we verify our token information:

```
it('should has token name and symbol', async () => {
  const tokenInfo = await token.tokenInfo();
  assert(tokenInfo[1]===name)
  assert(tokenInfo[2]===symbol)
})
it('should mint total supply of tokens to initial account', async () => {
  const initialAccountBalance = await token.balanceOf(initialAccount)
  assert(initialAccountBalance.eq(tokenTotalSupply))
})
```

The preceding test methods are used to test the token name and symbol. They also assert the total supply amount.

When a recipient is not in the `Whitelist`, the `transfer` and the `transferFrom` transaction should get reverted:

```
it('should revert transfers between non-whitelisted accounts', async ()
=> {
   let revertedTransfer = false
   try {
     await token.transfer(recipient, transferValue, { from: sender })
   } catch (err) {
     revertedTransfer = true
   }
   assert(revertedTransfer)
})

it('should revert use of transferFrom between non-whitelisted accounts',
async () => {
   let revertedTransfer = false
   try {
     await token.approve(owner, transferValue, { from: sender })
     await token.transferFrom(sender, recipient, transferValue, { from:
owner })
   } catch (err) {
     revertedTransfer = true
   }
   assert(revertedTransfer)
})
```

Since we have added the recipient to the `Whitelist`, the `detectTransferRestriction` method should detect restriction for transfer between `non-whitelisted` accounts.

The `messageForTransferRestriction` method will return the `NON_WHITELIST_ERROR` message for the `NON_WHITELIST_CODE`:

```
it('should detect restriction for transfer between non-whitelisted
accounts', async () => {
   const code = await token.detectTransferRestriction(sender, recipient,
transferValue)
   assert(code.eq(NON_WHITELIST_CODE))
})
it('should return non-whitelisted error message for whitelist error
code', async () => {
   const message = await
token.messageForTransferRestriction(NON_WHITELIST_CODE)
   assert.equal(NON_WHITELIST_ERROR, message)
})
```

The preceding test cases are for the non-whitelist restrict function. It verifies that the transfer in the ERC1404 smart contract is restricted in certain comply rules.

Next, we start to define test cases that add a recipient to the whitelist; in this case, the sender and recipient are both in the whitelist. The WhiteList function is used in the transfer and transferFrom functions to check whether the account is allowed to perform these actions.

Add a recipient to whitelist and then verify that the added recipient is in whitelist:

```
it('should allow contract owner to whitelist an account', async () => {
  await token.addAddressToWhitelist(operator, { from: owner })
  const operatorIsWhitelisted = await token.whitelist(operator)
  assert(operatorIsWhitelisted)
})
```

Since the recipient is in whitelist, rerun the transfer and transferFrom methods, and the amount transfer transaction between two accounts should happen:

```
it('should allow transfer between whitelisted accounts', async () => {
  await token.transfer(recipient, transferValue, { from: sender })
  const senderBalanceAfter = await token.balanceOf(sender)
  const recipientBalanceAfter = await token.balanceOf(recipient)
   assert.equal(
     senderBalanceAfter.valueOf(),
     senderBalanceBefore.minus(transferValue).valueOf()
   )
   assert.equal(
     recipientBalanceAfter.valueOf(),
     recipientBalanceBefore.plus(transferValue).valueOf()
   )
})
  it('should allow use of transferFrom between whitelisted accounts', async
() => {
    await token.approve(owner, transferValue, { from: sender })
    await token.transferFrom(sender, recipient, transferValue, { from:
owner })
    const senderBalanceAfter = await token.balanceOf(sender)
    const recipientBalanceAfter = await token.balanceOf(recipient)
    assert.equal(
      senderBalanceAfter.valueOf(),
      senderBalanceBefore.minus(transferValue).valueOf()
    )
    assert.equal(
```

```
        recipientBalanceAfter.valueOf(),
        recipientBalanceBefore.plus(transferValue).valueOf()
    )
})
```

Calling the `detectTransferRestriction` function should return a `SUCCESS_CODE`. The return code will be 0. The `messageForTransferRestriction` function will return a `SUCCESS_MESSAGE`. Here is the test case:

```
it('should detect success for valid transfer', async () => {
    const code = await token.detectTransferRestriction(sender, recipient,
transferValue)
    assert(code.eq(SUCCESS_CODE))
})
it('should ensure success code is 0', async () => {
    assert.equal(SUCCESS_CODE, 0)
})
it('should return success message for success code', async () => {
    const message = await token.messageForTransferRestriction(SUCCESS_CODE)
    assert.equal(SUCCESS_MESSAGE, message)
})
```

All right, we have finished writing all of the unit test cases for our ERC1404 token contract. Let's compile and test it.

Run the following `compile` command:

truffle compile

If you don't see a error during compilation, run all the test cases we just defined. Run the `test` command:

truffle test

If everything is fine, all our test cases should pass:

```
Contract: MyERC1404
  √ should has token name and symbol (44ms)
  √ should mint total supply of tokens to initial account
  √ should revert transfers between non-whitelisted accounts (39ms)
  √ should revert use of transferFrom between non-whitelisted accounts (123ms)
  √ should detect restriction for transfer between non-whitelisted accounts
  √ should return non-whitelisted error message for whitelist error code
  √ should allow contract owner to whitelist an account (98ms)
  √ should allow transfer between whitelisted accounts (141ms)
  √ should allow use of transferFrom betwen whitelisted accounts (222ms)
  √ should detect success for valid transfer
  √ should ensure success code is 0
  √ should return success message for success code
```

If you can run this, congratulations! We can start deploying our first ERC1404 security token on to the Ganache local network.

2_deploy_contracts.js under simple-restricted-token\migrations specifies which contract will deploy to the network, and it can also instantiate the smart contract from there. Let's add our ERC1404 smart contract there.

Open 2_deploy_contracts.js and add the following code. In function, we also pass the accounts argument to get the owner account for the token issuer:

```
var MyERC1404 = artifacts.require("./token/ERC1404/MyERC1404.sol");

module.exports = function (deployer, network, accounts)
  deployer.then(async () => {
    try {
....
      const ownerAddress = accounts[0];
      await deployer.deploy(MyERC1404, "myERC1404Token", "MYT1404",
ownerAddress, ' 50000000000000000000');
    } catch (err) {
      console.log(('Failed to Deploy Contracts', err))
    }
  })
}
```

We assign the first account as the `owner` account; the token name is `nyERC1404Token`, and the symbol is `MYR1404`. The `initialBalance` is 50 ether. Run `truffle migrate` to deploy our contract, as shown in the following screenshot:

```
     Migrations: 0xaca936995d556bdf21333c4f20e7616ea134ea5f
Saving successful migration to network...
    ... 0x8f3a621a34478b70c43e005d784caef463fcebf3b7bf3db96b7e72acc754c8af
Saving artifacts...
Running migration: 2_deploy_contracts.js
  Running step...
  Deploying MessagesAndCodes...
    ... 0x09b07834fd3261263a76829db20e74ff2cf03e00179f87e863f365ee33d62def
MessagesAndCodes: 0x23564a9a403ef622d12454d732f9906e8bc3a090
Linking MessagesAndCodes to IndivisibleTokenMock
Linking MessagesAndCodes to BasicWhitelistTokenMock
Linking MessagesAndCodes to ManagedWhitelistTokenMock
Linking MessagesAndCodes to MaxOwnershipStakeTokenMock
Linking MessagesAndCodes to MaxNumShareholdersTokenMock
Linking MessagesAndCodes to IndividualOwnershipStakeTokenMock
Linking MessagesAndCodes to ST20ExampleMock
Deploying MyERC1404...
    ... 0x5f5af354fd4bf309f56a346bb24afab347dd37f08babd07336e22add1e0ed8ce
MyERC1404: 0xc109f603b093dc21c6cf7a082c1cc5693909f7bc
Saving successful migration to network...
    ... 0x65661a738ad8599bc65beb8632791f1c5f3edaf4f700f232b0eaa059e8f3d170
Saving artifacts...
```

Let's learn to write Dapp web components.

Writing Dapp web components

We just deployed our `ERC1404` security token contract to the Ganache network. In this section, we will write the UI code to interact with the smart contact.

Ethereum provides the `web3.js` JavaScript API, which can connect to a local or remote blockchain node through HTTP or an **Interprocess Communication** (**IPC**) protocol. The API provides methods that allow a web client to interact with the Ethereum network.

The MetaMask Chrome extension is a very popular Ethereum browser tool that can provide a user-friendly interface; you can connect to a local or a remote blockchain environment and interact with a smart contract in the blockchain. If you have MetaMask installed, you can call it by using the following code:

```
if (typeof web3 !== 'undefined') {
  // Provided a web3 instance is provided already by Meta Mask.
  App.web3Provider = web3.currentProvider;
  web3 = new Web3(web3.currentProvider);
}
```

For our ERC1404, we just use a simple HttpProvider to connect to the Ganache server:

```
App.web3Provider = new
Web3.providers.HttpProvider('http://localhost:8545');
```

Setting up a Dapp project

The simple-restricted-token project is a Truffle-based project. Truffle provides a set of template files that can help us quickly start Dapp development. truffle-contract.js, which wraps around the web3.js API and handles a lot of heavy-lifting tasks for us, simplifies the use of the API provided by Truffle and directly interacts with a smart contract function. The simple-restricted-token currently only contains a smart contract library. We need to get more frontend files from other Truffle templates. Truffle boxes have many prebuild projects with helpful boilerplates. For our ERC1404 token Dapp development, we will use simple jQuery-based Truffle box boilerplates to start our web development.

Create any folder. Then, under the newly created folder, run the truffle unbox command:

```
Truffle unbox tutorialtoken
```

This will download the `tutorialtoken` truffle Dapp project:

```
D:\projects\sto\test>truffle unbox tutorialtoken

√ Preparing to download
√ Downloading
√ Cleaning up temporary files
√ Setting up box

Unbox successful. Sweet!

Commands:

   Compile:        truffle compile
   Migrate:        truffle migrate
   Test contracts: truffle test
   Run dev server: npm run dev
```

Let's look at the project boilerplates files. There is an `src` folder that contains a bunch of CSS, font, and `.js` files, including `web3.min.js`, `truffle-contract.js`, and so on. We need these files for our `ERC1404` Dapp projects:

We also need the `bs-config.json` file. The `tutorialtoken` project uses `lite-server` as a development web server. `lite-server` uses Browsersync, and `bs-config.js` will override configuration.

Moreover, provide `baseDir` so that `lite-server` can load UI files under the `src` folder and compile smart contract files under `build/contracts`:

```
{
  "server": {
    "baseDir": ["./src", "./build/contracts"]
  }
}
```

Copy the `src` folder and `bs-config.js` from the `tutorialtoken` project to the `simple-restricted-token` project.

You should get a simple project structure, as shown in the following screenshot:

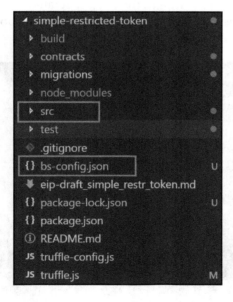

Then, we will install `lite-server`:

```
simple-restricted-token>npm install lite-server
```

This will set up our `lite-server`.

The last thing for the dev server's configuration is that we need to add the dev command to the package.json file, as follows:

```
"scripts": {
  "test": "truffle test",
..
  "dev": "lite-server"
},
```

When we run the npm run dev command, it will start our lite-dev-server.

Cleaning boilerplates code

The tutorialtoken project's index.html and app.js files have many unrelated codes for our projects; we need to clean up these files.

Open index.html and update the title to the project-related title. Remove all the contents under the <body> tag, that is, container. Moreover, add one bootstrap row for the content title:

```html
<title>ERC1404 Token Example</title>
<!-- Bootstrap -->
<link href="css/bootstrap.min.css" rel="stylesheet">
<!-- HTML5 shim and Respond.js for IE8 support of HTML5 elements and media queries -->
<!-- WARNING: Respond.js doesn't work if you view the page via file:// -->
<!--[if lt IE 9]>
  <script src="https://oss.maxcdn.com/html5shiv/3.7.3/html5shiv.min.js"></script>
  <script src="https://oss.maxcdn.com/respond/1.4.2/respond.min.js"></script>
<![endif]-->
</head>
<body>
  <div class="container">
    <div class="row">
      <div class="col-xs-12 col-sm-8 col-sm-push-2">
        <h1 class="text-center">ERC1404 Security Token</h1>
        <hr/>
        <br/>
      </div>
    </div>
  </div>
  <!-- jQuery (necessary for Bootstrap's JavaScript plugins) -->
  <script src="https://ajax.googleapis.com/ajax/libs/jquery/1.12.4/jquery.min.js"></script>
```

We will implement each function later. In `app.js`, let's clean up all the code and put in the following code template:

```
App = {
  web3Provider: null,
  contracts: {},
  init: function() {
    return App.initWeb3();
  },
  initWeb3: function() {
      App.web3Provider = new
Web3.providers.HttpProvider('http://127.0.0.1:8545');
      web3 = new Web3(App.web3Provider);
    return App.initContract();
  },
  initContract: function() {
  },
  bindEvents: function() {
  },
  handleTransfer: function(event) {
    event.preventDefault();
  },
  handleDetectTransferRestriction: function(event) {
    event.preventDefault();
  },
  handleMessageForTransferRestriction: function(event) {
  },
  handleAddAddressToWhitelist: function(event) {
    event.preventDefault();
  },
  handleVerifyWhitelistAddress: function(event) {
    event.preventDefault();
  }
};
$(function() {
  $(window).load(function() {
    App.init();
  });
});
```

If you have followed all the preceding steps, it is time to bring up our web page. Run the following command:

```
npm run dev
```

We get the following output:

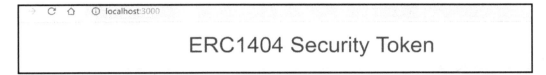

You can see that our page is displayed at localhost:3000.

Defining the HTML template

In this section, we will implement the ERC1404 UI component, which can interact with the smart contract that's been deployed in the Ganache network. We will define the following UI components: transfer, handleDetectTransferRestriction, messageForTransferRestriction, addAddressToWhitelist, and verifyWhitelist.

Here is the UI layout HTML code:

```
<div class="row">
    <div class="col-md-6"><div class="row">
        <ul class="nav nav-tabs" id="menuTabs">
<li class="active"><a data-toggle="tab" href="#transfer">transfer</a></li>
<li><a data-toggle="tab" href="#restriction">restriction</a></li>
<li><a data-toggle="tab"
href="#messageForTransferRestriction">message</a></li>
<li><a data-toggle="tab"
href="#addAddressToWhitelist">addWhitelist</a></li>
<li><a data-toggle="tab" href="#verifyWhitelist">verifyWhitelist</a></li>
        </ul>
        <div class="tab-content">
            <div id="transfer" class="tab-pane fade in active">
                <div class="panel-body">transfer</div></div>
            <div id="restriction" class="tab-pane fade">
                <div class="panel-body">restriction</div></div>
            <div id="messageForTransferRestriction" class="tab-pane fade">
                <div class="panel-
body">messageForTransferRestriction</div></div>
            <div id="addAddressToWhitelist" class="tab-pane fade">
                <div class="panel-body">addAddressToWhitelist</div></div>
            <div id="verifyWhitelist" class="tab-pane fade">
                <div class="panel-body">verifyWhitelist</div></div>
        </div></div></div>
    <div class="col-md-6"></div>
</div>
```

Open your web page; you will see the following:

Next, we also need load all Ganache default account and ERC1404 token information; we can put this information on the right-hand side of the page. Put the following HTML code on the right-hand side of `<div class="col-md-6"></div>`:

```
<div class="form-group  mb-2">
    <label for="exampleFormControlSelect1">ERC 1404 Token</label>
        <div class="input-group">
         <span class="input-group-addon"><a class="copy" data-clipboard-
target="#accts"><img class="clippy" src="images/clippy.svg" width="13"
alt="Copy to clipboard"></a></span>
        <select class="form-control" id="accts"></select>
        </div>
</div>
<table class="table table-hover table-striped">
    <tbody>
        <tr><th scope="row">Owner Address</th>
            <td><span class="text-info" id="address"></span></td>
        </tr>
        <tr><th scope="row">name</th>
            <td><span class="text-info" id="name"></span></td>
        </tr>
        <tr><th scope="row">symbol</th>
            <td><span class="text-info" id="symbol"></span></td>
        </tr>
        <tr><th scope="row">totalSupply</th>
            <td><span class="text-info" id="totalSupply"></span></td>
        </tr>
    </tbody>
</table>
```

This defines basic token information and accounts from Ganache.

For our contract account transfer and verification, we often need to copy different accounts as input addresses; we will use `clipboard.min.js` to help us copy and paste the address. Include the following script file in `index.html`:

```
<script
src="https://cdn.jsdelivr.net/npm/clipboard@2/dist/clipboard.min.js"></scri
pt>
```

At this point, you will see the following page in a browser:

Let's learn to implement the ERC1404 UI components.

Implementing the ERC1404 UI components

We will implement the UI components for `transfer`, `restriction`, `message`, `addwhiteList`, and `verifyWhiteList` in this section.

Loading accounts

Let's implement loading Ganache accounts to a web page. In `initContarct`, we load `MyERC1404.json`. If you remember, `bs-config.json` connects the project to load compiled contract files from `./build/contracts`. The `MyERC1404.json` file contains compiled `MyERC1404` smart contract information.

With the method provided from `truffle-contract.js`, we can read smart contract information from the blockchain:

```
initContract: function() {
  $.getJSON("MyERC1404.json", function(myERC1404) {
    // Instantiate a new truffle contract from the artifact
    App.contracts.MyERC1404 = TruffleContract(myERC1404);
    // Connect the provider in order to interact with contract
    App.contracts.MyERC1404.setProvider(App.web3Provider);
      return App.render();
  });
},
render: function() {
  var crowdFundingInstance;
  // Load account data
  var i =0;
  $('#accts').empty();
  web3.eth.accounts.forEach( function(e){
      $('#accts').append($('<option>', {
          value:e,
          text : e + " (" +web3.fromWei(web3.eth.getBalance(e), "ether")
+ " ether)"
      }));
  })
  App.contracts.MyERC1404.deployed().then(function(instance) {
    myERC1404Instance = instance;
    return myERC1404Instance.tokenInfo();
  }).then(function(tokenMeta) {
      $("#address").text(tokenMeta[0]);
      $("#name").text(tokenMeta[1]);
      $("#symbol").text(tokenMeta[2]);
      $("#totalSupply").text(tokenMeta[3]);
  }).catch(function(error) {
    console.warn(error);
    $("#error-msg").html(error).show();
  });
},
```

By looping through `web3.eth.accounts.forEach`, we will load all Ganache default accounts to our UI.

`App.contracts.MyERC1404.deployed()` will deploy an ERC1404 smart contract instance from blockchain, and read the smart contract function and variables. In the preceding code, we read `tokenInfo` from the `myERC1404` instance and displayed data in the UI:

Let's explore the `transfer` UI component.

transfer UI component

Let's implement the `transfer` UI component.

The UI needs to have `sender`, `recipient`, and `amount` to transfer components. We can reuse the right-hand side section of the previous page to select the `ERC 1404 Token` account list as the `sender`. So, we need to write a transfer to input the `recipient` address. To make it more user-friendly, we will use `ClipboardJS` to copy an address from the selected account list to the `recipient` address:

```
<form id="fund-form" method="post" role="form" style="display: block;">
    <div class="form-group row">
        <div class="row">
            <div class="col-lg-12">
                <input type="range" name="amtInputName" id="amtInputId"
value="0" min="1" max="100" oninput="amtOutputId.value = amtInputId.value">
                <div style="display: inline;"><output name="amtOutputName"
id="amtOutputId">0</output> <span>ether</span></div>
            </div>
        </div>
    </div>
    <div class="form-group row">
        <div class="col-lg-12">
            <label for="transferTo">To:</label>
```

```
            <input type="text" class="form-control" name="transferTo"
id="transferTo" value="">
            </div>
        </div>
    <div class="form-group">
        <div class="row">
            <div class="col-lg-12">
                <button type="button" id="transferToBtn" class="btn btn-success
pull-left">Transfer</button>
            </div>
        </div>
    </div>
</form>
```

If the `recipient` is not in `whitelist`, we will get a restriction message, and we need a place to display these messages:

```
        <div id="success-msg" class="row text-center alert alert-
success"></div>
        <div id="error-msg" class="row text-center alert alert-danger">
</div>
```

In `app.js`, let's implement the copy logic and the transfer logic.

Copy the clipboard logic:

```
var clipboard = new ClipboardJS('.copy');
clipboard.on('success', function(e) {
  let activeTab = $("ul#menuTabs li.active a").text();
  if('restriction'===activeTab) {
    $('#recipient').val(e.text);
  } else if('addWhitelist'===activeTab) {
    $('#addWhiteListAddress').val(e.text);
  } else if('verifyWhitelist'===activeTab) {
    $('#inputWhiteListAddress').val(e.text);
  }
});
```

For the transfer logic, we read the `sender` and `recipient` address and put in the amount to call the `transfer` method in the smart contract; since the recipient is a non-whitelist, we should see an error revert message:

```
handleTransfer: function(event) {
  event.preventDefault();
  cleanMsg();
  var sender = $('#accts').find(":selected").val();
  var transferValue = $('#amtOutputId').val();
  var recipient = $('#transferTo').val();
```

```
        let message ="";
        const transferValueInWei = web3.toWei(transferValue, 'ether');
        App.contracts.MyERC1404.deployed().then(function(newInstance) {
          return newInstance.balanceOf(recipient);
        }).then(function(recipientValue) {
          message ="ERC1404 recipient amount (before): "
    +web3.fromWei(recipientValue, "ether") + " ether";
        });
        App.contracts.MyERC1404.deployed().then(function(instance) {
          return instance.transfer(recipient, transferValueInWei, {from:
    sender, gas:3500000});
        }).then(function(result) {
          App.contracts.MyERC1404.deployed().then(function(newInstance) {
            return newInstance.balanceOf(recipient);
          }).then(function(recipientValue) {
            $("#success-msg").html(message+ "<br/> ERC1404 recipient amount
    (after): " +web3.fromWei(recipientValue, "ether") + " ether"  ).show();
          });
        }).catch(function(err) {
          console.error(err);
          $("#error-msg").html(err).show();
        });
      },
```

Copy the second account from the account list, and click the **Copy** button. This will copy the selected account to the recipient's input field.

Then, select the transfer amount, and select the owner's account as the sender. Click **Transfer** to get the following output:

Let's explore the `DetectTransferRestriction` UI component.

DetectTransferRestriction UI component

We just implemented the `transfer` UI logic. `DetectTransferRestriction` is quite similar to the `transfer` UI, which needs one recipient input, the `amount` field, and **Submit** button.

In `handleDetectTransferRestriction`, we call `detectTransferRestriction` by passing all the necessary parameters that are similar to the `transfer` function. The method returns code. For display usage, we use `messageForTransferRestriction` to display the related human-readable message. These components show the `detectTransferRestriction` and `messageForTransferRestriction` functions.

Here is the implementation for `handleDetectTransferRestriction`:

```
handleDetectTransferRestriction: function(event) {
  event.preventDefault();
  cleanMsg();
  var sender = $('#accts').find(":selected").val();
  var transferValue =  $('#amtOutputTransferRestriction').val();
  var recipient = $('#recipient').val();
  const transferValueInWei = web3.toWei(transferValue, 'ether');
  App.contracts.MyERC1404.deployed().then(function(instance) {
    return instance.detectTransferRestriction(sender, recipient,
transferValueInWei, {  gas:3500000});
  }).then(function(code) {
    App.contracts.MyERC1404.deployed().then(function(newInstance) {
      return newInstance.messageForTransferRestriction(code);
    }).then(function(message) {
      if('SUCCESS'===message) {
        $("#success-msg").html("ERC1404 Message: " + message ).show();
      } else {
        $("#error-msg").html("ERC1404 Message: " + message ).show();
      }
    });
  }).catch(function(err) {
    console.error(err);
    $("#error-msg").html(err).show();
  });
}
```

Here is the UI for this component:

Let's explore the `MessageForTransferRestriction` UI component.

MessageForTransferRestriction UI component

In `DetectTransferRestriction`, we call both the `messageForTransferRestriction` and `DetectTransferRestriction` methods. This tab just simply shows how we use `messageForTransferRestriction` to display messages. It is quite simple. We just need a button to call the `message` function and a place to display the message. Here is the implementation for the `handleMessageForTransferRestriction` function:

```
App.contracts.MyERC1404.deployed().then(function(instance) {
    return instance.NON_WHITELIST_CODE();
}).then(function(result) {
    App.contracts.MyERC1404.deployed().then(function(newInstance) {
        return newInstance.messageForTransferRestriction(result);
    }).then(function(message) {
        $("#restrictionMsg").html(message);
    });
```

By clicking the **messageForTransferRestriction** button, we can see the following page result:

Let's explore the `AddAddressToWhitelist` UI component.

AddAddressToWhitelist UI component

We have developed and tested the `transfer`, `messageForTransferRestriction`, and `DetectTransferRestriction` UI components for the non-whitelist case. Now, let's work on implementing the `addWhitelist` UI component.

The UI should be quite straightforward: provide a component and let the token issuer add a recipient to the `whitelist` address. Moreover, use the **Submit** button to add an address to `whitelist`:

```
<form id="fund-form" method="post" role="form" style="display: block;">
    <div class="form-group row">
        <div class="form-group row">
            <div class="col-lg-12">
            <label for="addWhiteListAddress">Add To White List</label>
            <input type="text" class="form-control"
name="addWhiteListAddress" id="addWhiteListAddress" value="">
            </div>
        </div>
        <div class="row">
            <div class="col-lg-12">
             <span><button type="button" id="addWhiteListBtn" class="btn btn-sm
btn-success">Submit</button></span>
            </div>
        </div>
    </div>
</form>
```

The `handleAddAddressToWhitelist` script logic will call
`addAddressToWhitelist(operator, { from: sender, gas:3500000})` by passing
the recipient. Once this is done, we will display a message on the page:

```
handleAddAddressToWhitelist: function(event) {
    event.preventDefault();
    cleanMsg();
    var operator = $('#addWhiteListAddress').val();
    var sender = $('#accts').find(":selected").val();
    App.contracts.MyERC1404.deployed().then(function(instance) {
        return instance.addAddressToWhitelist(operator, { from: sender,
gas:3500000});
    }).then(function(result) {
        $("#success-msg").html("Success add " + operator + " to white
List").show();
    }).catch(function(err) {
        console.error(err);
        $("#error-msg").html(err).show();
    });
},
```

Let's add one address (the second account) to `whitelist`.

If we use the third account as `sender`, the transaction for `addWhiteList` will be rejected,
since the third account doesn't have permission:

Only the `owner` account has permission:

Let's explore the `verifyWhitelist` UI component.

verifyWhitelist UI component

We added the second account to the `whitelist`; let's call the `whitelist(address)` function to verify it. In our UI component, we simply write an input address and press the **Submit** button.

In the `handleVerifyWhitelistAddress` script logic, we call the `whitelist` smart contract function. Moreover, we display the returned result to the user:

```
          handleVerifyWhitelistAddress: function(event) {
      event.preventDefault();
      cleanMsg();
      var operator =  $('#inputWhiteListAddress').val();
      App.contracts.MyERC1404.deployed().then(function(instance) {
        return instance.whitelist(operator, { gas:3500000});
      }).then(function(result) {
        if(result) {
          $("#success-msg").html("The Address: " + operator + " is in white
List").show();
        } else {
          $("#error-msg").html("The Address: " + operator + " is not in white
List").show();
        }

      }).catch(function(err) {
```

```
        console.error(err);
        $("#error-msg").html(err).show();
    });
}
```

The following screenshot shows verification of the second address by the owner:

The owner would run the code again and verify the third address. Since the third address is non-whitelist, we will see NON_WHITELIST_MESSAGE:

Finally, let's run our `transfer` function between the two `whitelist` accounts. For our case, it is the first and second account. It should execute by the token issuer account (the first). Transfer an amount, and click **Transfer**:

As expected, the amount gets transferred successfully from one account to the second account, as shown in the following screenshot:

```
eth_sendTransaction

    Transaction: 0x01d9f3a5bb4dfbf03e48e4804a22425ba9a8811215aa98059e9433f7f300c31a
    Gas usage: 38294
    Block Number: 18
    Block Time: Sat Mar 09 2019 03:29:34 GMT-0500 (Eastern Standard Time)

eth_getTransactionReceipt
eth_call
```

In the preceding screenshot, you can also see the transaction log in the Ganache console.

Summary

In this chapter, we learned how to build our ERC1404 security token from a smart contract to Dapp. Now, we should have a very basic understanding of a security token smart contract. In the real world, a security token will be far more complex than in this example. Many security tokens run on a complex ecosystem and need to comply with the **Securities and Exchange Commission's (SEC's)** regulations regarding securities trading. The smart contract needs to incorporate a real-world, large number of legal contracts.

In the next chapter, Chapter 7, *Stablecoin Smart Contracts,* we will talk about a stablecoin smart contract in detail.

Stablecoin Smart Contracts

7

We covered the basics of stablecoins in `Chapter 4`, *Stablecoin*. We learned what stablecoins are, why we need then, their basic types, and their challenges. In this chapter, we will explore more about these primary stablecoins, including how blockchain technologies help cryptocurrency tokens to minimize price volatility. This chapter is split into two major topics, as follows:

- Quick primary stablecoin overview
- Stablecoin technical design overview

Quick primary stablecoin overview

Stablecoins play an important role in the digital asset world. One of the major designs of stablecoins is to minimize digital currency price volatility. In the past couple of years, the most popular cryptocurrency prices have been very volatile, for example, bitcoin and Ethereum. Huge price fluctuations prevent the wide adoption of cryptocurrency as money for daily transactions. That is where stablecoins are designed to address this issue.

As we learned in `Chapter 4`, *Stablecoin*, stablecoins connect cryptocurrency and fiat currencies with the total amount of backed assets (mostly, this is in USD, or in a digit currency such as bitcoin, ether, or gold). It stabilizes the price with the one-to-one equivalent in USD, euros, or cryptocurrency.

Timeline of stablecoin development

In the past few years, many stablecoin projects have been launched in the cryptocurrency market. The following diagram shows a timeline of the launches of primary stablecoins in the last few years:

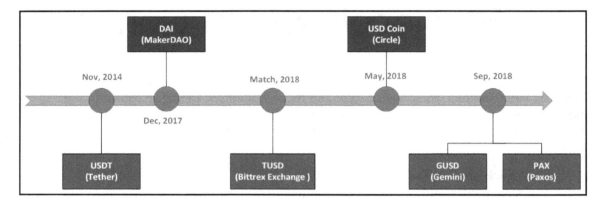

Tether is the most popular stablecoin in the current market. Every **Tether** coin (**USDT**) is backed by USD in a 1:1 ratio. This means that the value of **USDT** is equal to the value of the USD. The **USDT** was built on Omni and launched in November, 2014.

MakerDAO is a fully decentralized solution. It issues a stablecoin known as **Dai**. Similar to **Tether**, **Dai** tied is with the US dollar with a ratio of 1:0 and is backed by multiple assets. **Dai** is collateralized by ether. MakerDAO was launched in December, 2017.

TUSD is similar to **Tether** and is a USD-backed stablecoin, which aims for a 1:1 ratio with USD. A user can redeem 1 **TUSD** for $1. The beauty of **TUSD** is its transparency. It is built on the Ethereum blockchain, and its decentralized features mean that anyone can access the regular attestations of escrowed balances. **TUSD** also provides legal protection for the token holder. **TUSD** was launched in March, 2018 at the Bittrex exchange.

USD Coin (USDC) was launched by Circle Internet Financial Limited and the CENTRE open source consortium in May, 2018. Like most of the other stablecoins, it was backed by USD and aims for a 1:1 ratio between USDC and USD. USDC is an ERC-20 token that runs on Ethereum. Third-party professional services such as Grant Thornton help to verify Circle's backed USD. It makes stablecoins more transparent and trustworthy. It also provides legal protection for the token holder.

PAX and **GUSD** were known as the regulated stablecoins. In September 2018, both stablecoins were approved by the **New York State Department of Financial Services** (**NYSDFS**). **PAX** and **GUSD** are both ERC-20 tokens that are run on Ethereum blockchain.

The **Gemini dollar (GUSD)** was issued by Gemini Trust Company LLC. The traditional fiat USD are kept in reserve in the State Street Bank and other trust companies. One GUSD is equal to $1. The professional third-party company will continue to monitor the **GUSD** smart contract code. Independently registered public accounting firms perform attestations for US dollar-backed bank accounts on a monthly basis to ensure balance consistency.

1 **PAX** is equal to $1. This is held in a dedicated omnibus cash account in an FDID-insured State Street Bank and other trust companies. The top public auditing firm (Withum) regularly runs audits for these accounts to increase public transparency and trustworthiness.

Types of stablecoin

As we learned in Chapter 4, *Stablecoin*, there are several types of stablecoins. At a high level, there are three major types:

- **Fiat Collateralized**
- **Crypto Collateralized**
- **Non-Collateralized**

The following diagram shows the major three types of stablecoin:

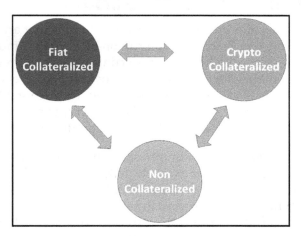

Let's look at them in detail.

Fiat collateralized stablecoins

Fiat collateralized stablecoins are backed by gold or fiat currencies such as the US dollar, euro, and so on. The token aims to keep a 1:1 ratio with the underlying asset. The token holder can redeem assets at any time with a stable 1:1 price peg. The centralized entity has to maintain a relative level of stability. This solution is a more off-the-chain centralized solution.

Tether and USDC belong to this type of stablecoin. When the user buys stablecoin using dollars, this will be put into a bank account and will be left untouched. When the token holder wants to redeem the stablecoin back into dollars, the extra amount of stablecoins will be burned by the system.

Since it is a centralized solution, the entire process is not fully transparent. This off-the-chain solution is criticized as having high counterparty risk. The off-the-chain legacy payment process is slow and time-consuming. Since more and more regulated compliant requirements were requested by the government and the industry, many fiat collateralized stablecoins make efforts to make their assets more transparent and auditable by providing sufficient data to cover critical **I owe you** (**IOU**). The advance of a fiat-backed stablecoin is that it is 100% price stable and simple.

Crypto collateralized stablecoins

Crypto collateralized stablecoins are decentralized stablecoins that are backed by crypto assets such as ether and bitcoin. Stablecoin can run on blockchains, mostly Ethereum-based ones. This type of token is typically ERC-20 smart contract-based. It relies on on-the-chain trustless insurance to maintain coin price stability. Since cryptocurrency prices fluctuate over time, crypto collateralized stablecoin needs to keep the price stable. The way to resolve this is by using over-collateralized stablecoin. When the crypto asset price drops, the stablecoins can absorb price fluctuations and become liquidated.

With proper smart contract logic, the entire process can be automatically controlled in a decentralized and transparent way. For example, let's say a token issuer deposits $20,000 for ether, then issues 10,000 stablecoins with a 1:1 ratio to USD. The stablecoin will over-collateralize for 200%. When the price drops, the stablecoin starts liquidating ETH collateral, so the value of the stablecoin still keeps a 1:1 ratio with USD. Since it is completely decentralized in a transparent way, the asset is locked up in the blockchain smart contract.

Compared to fiat-collateralized stablecoins, these stablecoins don't have trust issues. However, the complex smart contract is vulnerable to hacks. When the crypto asset price crashes hard enough, the maintenance for the peg of the price of stablecoins could fail. Over-collateralized management makes capital utilization inefficient.

Non-collateralized stablecoins

Non-collateralized stablecoins are also referred to as algorithmic stablecoins, seigniorage shares, decentralized bank, and future growth-backed stablecoins. It has no collateral-backed issuance.

It relies on an algorithm to change the volume of the token supply to control the token price's stability, just like a central bank maintains currency stability through the volume of currency it supplies. The smart contract will increase the token supply when the token market value increases and the lower price back to the peg.

On the other hand, when the stablecoin's price drops, the smart contract will provide **shares**. These shares offer a certain number of future growths to increase the capital per peg. By this way, the token keeps it as a stable price and maintains its peg.

Since this stablecoin uses a smart contract to handle token supply, it increases trust and transparency. No collateral-backed design makes it independent of centralization. The disadvantage of this approach is that, by increasing the complexity of a smart contract, the system is vulnerable to crashes; the participant is only incentivized based on the promise of future growth. When the prices slip down and coin demand decreases, it will be very hard to maintain its peg.

The following is a list of some stablecoins that fit into these three types of stablecoins:

Type	stablecoin
Fiat collateralized stablecoins	USDT and TUSD
Crypto collateralized stablecoins	DAI (MarkDAO) and BTS
Non-collateralized stablecoins	BASIS and CARBON

Stablecoin technical design overview

In this section, we will review the technical design of some major stablecoins, especially smart contracts.

Tether (USDT)

Tether stablecoins run on the bitcoin blockchain. These are designed in three layers, as shown in the following diagram:

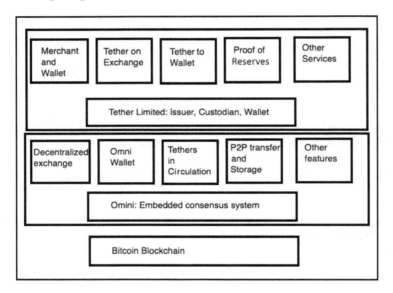

Let's take a look at these layers:

- **Bitcoin Blockchain**: Tether uses an embedded Omni consensus protocol to record Omni transactions in bitcoin transactions. Each Omni transaction has the same hash value in the blockchain.

- **Omni layer protocol**: It includes **Decentralized exchange, Omni Wallet, Tethers in Circulation, P2P transfer and storage**, and **Other features**. Tether protocol can create the token and redeem the token from the circulation supply and destroy USDT from the **Omni Wallet**. The Omnicore API and **OMNIEXPLORER.INFO** are used to track and display information about tether transactions and coin circulation. The **P2P transfer And Storage** and **Omni Wallet** features provide security environments for users so that they can transfer and store tethers and exchange assets or tokens.

Here is the **OMNIEXPLORER.INFO** site, which shows a tether's transaction information:

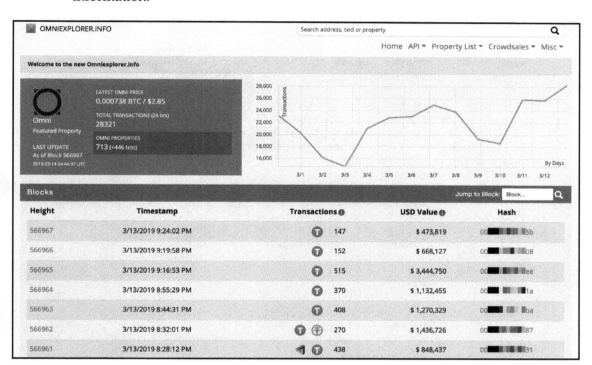

- **Tether Limited**: The top layer is **Tether Limited**, which is open for the business entity: **Issuer**, **Custodian**, and **Wallet**. This tier includes **Merchant and Wallet**, **Tether on Exchange**, **Tether to Wallet**, **Proof of Reserves**, and **Other Services**. These services can reserve custody fiat tokens with backed USDT in circulation, accept and deposit user fiat tokens and exchange the USDT stablecoins, return fiat to the user, and destroy the corresponding tethers. The user can use the wallet to send, receive, store, and convert USDT.

In November 2017, tether released both USD and euro Ethereum ERC-20 tokens via the Omni layer protocol. The token runs on Ethereum blockchain:

```
contract TetherToken is Pausable, StandardToken {
  ...
    function TetherToken(uint _initialSupply, string _name, string _symbol,
uint _decimals){}
    function transfer(address _to, uint _value) whenNotPaused {}
    function transferFrom(address _from, address _to, uint _value)
whenNotPaused {}
```

```
    function balanceOf(address who) constant returns (uint){}
    function approve(address _spender, uint _value) onlyPayloadSize(2 * 32)
{}
    function allowance(address _owner, address _spender) constant returns
(uint remaining) {}
    function deprecate(address _upgradedAddress) onlyOwner {
        deprecated = true;  upgradedAddress = _upgradedAddress;
        Deprecate(_upgradedAddress);
    }
    function totalSupply() constant returns (uint){}
    function issue(uint amount) onlyOwner {
        if (_totalSupply + amount < _totalSupply) throw;
        if (balances[owner] + amount < balances[owner]) throw;
        balances[owner] += amount;
        _totalSupply += amount;
        Issue(amount);
    }
    function redeem(uint amount) onlyOwner {
        if (_totalSupply < amount) throw;
        if (balances[owner] < amount) throw;
        _totalSupply -= amount;
        balances[owner] -= amount;
        Redeem(amount);
    }
    function setParams(uint newBasisPoints, uint newMaxFee) onlyOwner {
        if (newBasisPoints > 20) throw;
        if (newMaxFee > 50) throw;
        basisPointsRate = newBasisPoints;
        maximumFee = newMaxFee.mul(10**decimals);
        Params(basisPointsRate, maximumFee);
    }
    ..
}
```

TetherToken implements the ERC-20 token interface and includes transfer, approve, transferFrom, balanceOf, and allowance. In these methods, a TetherToken smart contract handles upgrades regarding the contract when it is deprecated.

It also defines stablecoin-related functions such as redeem, issue, deprecate, and setParms, as follows:

- Redeem(): When the user redeems their tokens, the function makes sure that the account has enough money in it before this token withdraws from the owner address or the call will fail
- Issue(): Issues new USDT tokens and deposits them into the user's account

- `Deprecate()`: Upgrades to a new contract address and deprecates the current contract
- `setParams()`: Applies rules to make sure that `newBasisPoints` and `newMaxFee` will be under certain limits

`TetherToken` extends the OpenZeppelin `Pausable` smart contract, which allows token owners to deliver upgrades and gives them the ability to perform an emergency stop mechanism when needed.

TrueUSD (TUSD) smart contract

TrueUSD manages the stablecoin smart contracts on their system. It has a high-level layout for TUSD smart contracts. The token is ERC-20 token-based.

TUSD's smart contract design is shown in the following diagram:

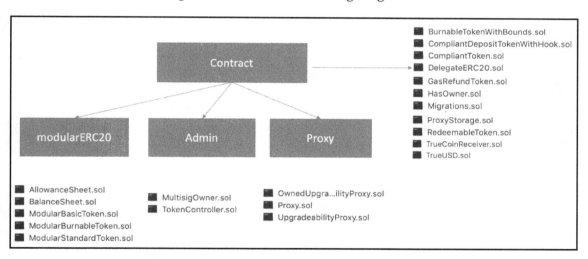

The contract contains the **modularERC20**, **Admin**, and **Proxy** packages, as well as main token contracts.

modularERC20

This folder contains a list of ERC-20 tokens related to the contract library; it is similar to OpenZeppelin. These contracts help to keep track of balance and allowances:

- `AllowanceSheet.sol`: This is a wrapper class for the `allowanceOf` mapping. The class provides the `addAllowance`, `subAllowance`, and `setAllowance` methods so that you can keep track of the allowance.
- `BalanceSheet.sol`: This is a wrapper class for the `balanceOf` mapping. The class provides the `addBalance`, `subBalance`, and `setBalance` methods so that you can keep track of the balance.
- `ModularBasicToken.sol`: This class is similar to OpenZeppelin's `BasicToken`. It uses the `BalanceSheet` contract to handle the `balanceOf` function.
- `ModularBurnableToken.sol`: This class provides a function to burn (destroy) specific amounts of tokens.
- `ModularStandardToken.sol`: This extends from `ModularBasicToken` and implements the basic standard token.

Proxy

The contracts in this folder use the proxy pattern and provide placeholders to delete the contract call to a given implementation:

- `Proxy.sol`: This provides a `fallback` method to delegate a function call to whatever the actual implementation is.
- `UpgradeabilityProxy.sol`: This class implements the `_setImplementation` and `_upgradeTo` methods. This class will manage the proxy implementation address (set and upgrade) and delete proxy calls to the implementation address.
- `OwnedUpgradeabilityProxy.sol`: This class extends from `UpgradeabilityProxy` and adds additional basic authorization control for contract functions.

The proxy contract combines an upgradability proxy with defining basic authorization ownership, such as `onlyProxyOwner` and `onlyPendingProxyOwner`.

Admin

The admin contracts provide admin functions to control token transfer, approve it, reject it, and so on:

- `MultisigOwner.sol`: This contract is responsible for invoking a function that has `onlyOwner` defined in `TokenController`, for example, `transferTusdProxyOwnership`, `claimTusdProxyOwnership`, `setMintLimits`, `transferMintKey`, and so on. This class is a placeholder class that delegates calls to `TokenController` with admin control.
  The `MultiSigOwner` contract has three owners. Each owner can only approve/reject the current action once. To veto the action, it requires 2/3 of the owners to act.
- `TokenController.sol`: This contract is an actual implementation for the proxy. The contract allows a TUSD contract to split ownership into two address: owner address and admin address.

The owner can mint new tokens and transfer ownership of the contract. An admin address has three types of address: `MintKey`, `MintRatifier`, and `MintPauser`. They are used to request, revoke, pause, and approve mints. There are three level of mints defined in this class, and they are `instantMint`, `ratifiedMint`, and `multiSigMint`. Each type of mint has its own threshold.

Other TUSD token-related contracts

Here are a few other smart contracts that are defined in a TrueUSD token system:

- `BurnableTokenWithBounds.sol`: This contract defines the minimum and maximum number of tokens that can be burned, and keeps track of these burns coins.
- `CompliantToken.sol`: This contract applies security KYC/AML checks to make sure that the token follows the regulated comply rule. Moreover, it is able to add bad actors to the blacklist.
- `RedeemableToken.sol`: This burns tokens by sending them to 0X0 (when the address is 0X0, it's impossible to generate the private key for this address).
- `GasRefundToken.sol`: This contract allows the user to sponsor gas refunds for transfer and mints and reduces the gas cost for mint and transfer.

Now, let's take a look at the `TrueUSD` contract:

```
contract TrueUSD is CompliantDepositTokenWithHook,
BurnableTokenWithBounds,
 RedeemableToken, DelegateERC20, GasRefundToken {
    function decimals() public pure returns (uint8) { return DECIMALS; }
    function rounding() public pure returns (uint8) { return ROUNDING; }
    function changeTokenName(string _name, string _symbol) external
onlyOwner {
        name = _name; symbol = _symbol;
        emit ChangeTokenName(_name, _symbol);
    }
    function reclaimEther(address _to) external onlyOwner {
        _to.transfer(address(this).balance);
    }
    function reclaimToken(ERC20 token, address _to) external onlyOwner {
        uint256 balance = token.balanceOf(this);
        token.transfer(_to, balance);
    }
    function paused() public pure returns (bool) { return false; }
    function reclaimContract(Ownable _ownable) external onlyOwner {
        _ownable.transferOwnership(owner);
    }
    function _burnAllArgs(address _burner, uint256 _value) internal {
        uint burnAmount = _value.div(10 ** uint256(DECIMALS -
ROUNDING)).mul(10 ** uint256(DECIMALS - ROUNDING));
        super._burnAllArgs(_burner, burnAmount);
    }
}
```

The `TrueUSD` contract class is the top level of the ERC-20 contract. It defines the most important functions:

- `reclaimToken`: Sends TUSD token balance to another address
- `reclaimEther`: Sends ETH balance from the contract account to another address
- `reclaimContract`: Allows the TUSD owner to reclaim ownership that is owned by any TUSD owned contract
- `_burnAllArgs`: Keeps track of the amount of burned coin and money that has been redeemed from the system

MakerDAO (Dai)

Maker is a **decentralized autonomous organization** (**DAO**) for the Ethereum blockchain. MakerDAO provides two coins: Maker coin (MKR) and Dai (DAI). The MKR is a system token that is used for the Maker platform. It is not a stablecoin. Dai is a stablecoin and is used for payment, collateral, exchange for the asset, and so on.

DSTokenBase implements ERC20 tokens. DSStop extends from DSNote and DSAuth.

DSAuth defines a token authority function. DSNote provides a callback to log token transaction information. In DSStop, it has the start and stop functions to help the token issuer to manage token transfer when it is needed.

Here is its implementation:

```
contract DSStop is DSNote, DSAuth {
bool public stopped;
  modifier stoppable {
        require(!stopped);
        _;
    }
    function stop() public auth note {
        stopped = true;
    }
    function start() public auth note {
        stopped = false;
    }
}
```

DSToken extends from DSTokenBase and DSStop. It provides all DSTokenBase ERC-20 token functions.

All of these functions are stoppable:

```
contract DSToken is DSTokenBase(0), DSStop {
    event Mint(address indexed guy, uint wad);
    event Burn(address indexed guy, uint wad);
    function approve(address guy) public stoppable returns (bool) {}
    function approve(address guy, uint wad) public stoppable returns (bool)
{}
    function transferFrom(address src, address dst, uint wad)  public
stoppable returns (bool) {
    function push(address dst, uint wad) public { transferFrom(msg.sender,
dst, wad); }
    function pull(address src, uint wad) public {transferFrom(src,
msg.sender, wad); }
    function move(address src, address dst, uint wad) public {
```

```
transferFrom(src, dst, wad);}
    function mint(uint wad) public { mint(msg.sender, wad); }
    function burn(uint wad) public {burn(msg.sender, wad); }
    function mint(address guy, uint wad) public auth stoppable {
        _balances[guy] = add(_balances[guy], wad);
        _supply = add(_supply, wad);
        emit Mint(guy, wad);
    }
    function burn(address guy, uint wad) public auth stoppable {
        if (guy != msg.sender && _approvals[guy][msg.sender] != uint(-1)) {
            _approvals[guy][msg.sender] = sub(_approvals[guy][msg.sender],
wad);
        }
        _balances[guy] = sub(_balances[guy], wad);
        _supply = sub(_supply, wad);
        emit Burn(guy, wad);
    }
}
```

By using the `burn()` and `mint()` functions, the platform can maintain its 1:1 peg to USD. `mint()` and `burn()` are tracked in the blockchain transaction. In the MakerDAO platform, the entire process is as follows:

1. The user creates the **collateralized debt position (CDP)** and locks up their ether in CDPs in the form of **Pooled Ether (PETH)**.
2. CDP generates the amount of Dai and deposits it into the user wallet while calculating interest over time.
3. The user redeems the collateral and pays the Dai, plus some amount for the stability fee (MKR) to the CDP. Once the user has paid the debt and stability fee, the CDP becomes debt-free.
4. The user gets their collateral back, and these Dais are burned. Then, the CDP is closed.

The following diagram displays the entire CDP flow:

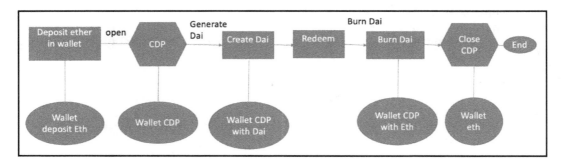

Now, we will take a look at USD coin.

USD coin (USDC)

USDC from the CENTRE consortium and Circle is an ERC-20 token. This stablecoin, like its counterparts, maintains a 1:1 ratio to USD and is guaranteed to be redeemed any time as USD when the user requests it. The token is audited monthly by independent certified third parties.

USDT uses the proxy pattern to upgrade versions of contract implementation. It uses the `zos-lib` library, `AdminUpgradeabilityProxy`, to manage `FiatTokenProxy` implementation when upgrading the version.

The following is the smart contract hierarchic diagram for USDC:

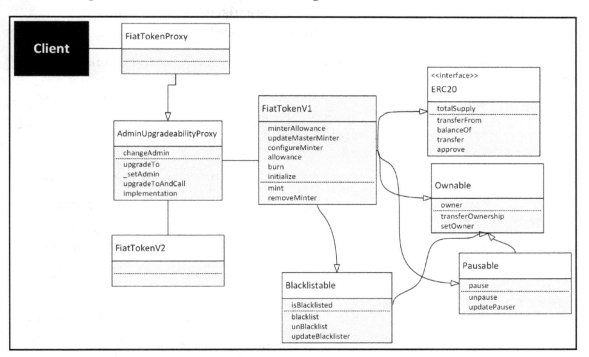

The **FiatTokenProxy** class extends from **AdminUpgradeabilityProxy** to call a different version of fiat token.

The **AdminUpgradeabilityProxy** smart contract has **upgradeTo**, which allows admins to upgrade the backing implementation of the proxy. **upgradeToAndCall** is quite useful for upgrading and initializing the proxied contract and to call a function. Only the proxy owner can change the proxy owner address:

- `Blacklistable.sol`: This allows admins to add accounts so that they can be blacklisted or removed from the blacklist.
- `blacklist()`: This adds accounts to the blacklist. When an address is in a blacklist, the USDC contract will prevent the address from transferring or receiving tokens.
- `unBlacklist()`: This removes an account from the blacklist.
- `Pausable.sol`: This allows the owner to pause and trigger a stopped state in an emergency case, for example, a contract security issue, a serious bug, and so on. When a contract is in a paused state, no transfer is allowed.
- `pause()`: This allows the owner to pause a trigger's stopped state.
- `unpause()`: The owner can return a pause state to its normal state.

USDT `FiatTokenV1` extends from the `Ownable`, `ERC20`, `Pausable`, and `Blacklistable` smart contracts.

Here is a `FiatTokenV1` contract:

```
contract FiatTokenV1 is Ownable, ERC20, Pausable, Blacklistable {
...
    function initialize(
        string _name, string _symbol, string _currency, uint8 _decimals,
address _masterMinter,
        address _pauser, address _blacklister, address _owner ) public {}
    modifier onlyMinters() {}
    function mint(address _to, uint256 _amount) whenNotPaused onlyMinters
notBlacklisted(msg.sender) notBlacklisted(_to) public returns (bool) {}
    modifier onlyMasterMinter() {}
    function minterAllowance(address minter) public view returns (uint256)
{}
    function isMinter(address account) public view returns (bool) {}
    function allowance(address owner, address spender) public view returns
(uint256) {}
    function totalSupply() public view returns (uint256) {}
    function balanceOf(address account) public view returns (uint256) {}
    function approve(address _spender, uint256 _value) whenNotPaused
notBlacklisted(msg.sender) notBlacklisted(_spender) public returns (bool)
{}
    function transferFrom(address _from, address _to, uint256 _value)
whenNotPaused notBlacklisted(_to) notBlacklisted(msg.sender)
```

```
notBlacklisted(_from) public returns (bool) {}
    function transfer(address _to, uint256 _value) whenNotPaused
notBlacklisted(msg.sender) notBlacklisted(_to) public returns (bool) {}
    function configureMinter(address minter, uint256 minterAllowedAmount)
whenNotPaused onlyMasterMinter public returns (bool) {}
   function removeMinter(address minter) onlyMasterMinter public returns
(bool) {}
    function burn(uint256 _amount) whenNotPaused onlyMinters
notBlacklisted(msg.sender) public {}
function updateMasterMinter(address _newMasterMinter) onlyOwner public {}
    }
```

Here's a summary of its functions:

- `mint()`: This function mints USDT tokens. When the minter mints new tokens, their allowance will decrease. When it gets too low, `masterMinter` can increase the allowance.
- `minterAllowance()`: This gets the minter allowance for an account.
- `configureMinter()`: This allows the `MasterMinter` to add/update a new minter when it is not paused. `MasterMinter` can add multiple minters to its control list.
- `removeMinter()`: This allows the `MasterMinter` to remove a minter.
- `burn()`: This allows a miner to burn a certain amount of tokens when it is not paused and when the minter is not blacklisted.
- `updateMasterMinter()`: This allows the contract owner to update `MasterMinter`.

Paxos Standard

Paxos Standard (**PAX**) has been approved by the NYSDFS. The token is backed by the US dollar and available in a 1:1 exchange ratio for USD.

All of these USD are deposited into FDIC-insured US banks or collateralized by US government treasuries. PAX is an ERC-20 token. The Paxos system minted and burned PAX in the life circle of the PAX token.

Let's take a look at the smart contract implementation of PAXImplementation:

```
contract PAXImplementation {
...
    function initialize() public {}
function totalSupply() public view returns (uint256) {}
    function transfer(address _to, uint256 _value) public whenNotPaused
returns (bool) {}
    function balanceOf(address _addr) public view returns (uint256) {}
    function transferFrom(address _from, address _to, uint256 _value
) public whenNotPaused returns (bool) {}
    function approve(address _spender, uint256 _value) public whenNotPaused
returns (bool) {}
    function allowance(address _owner, address _spender) public
    view returns (uint256) {}
    modifier onlyOwner() {}
    function transferOwnership(address _newOwner) public onlyOwner {}
    modifier whenNotPaused() {}
    function pause() public onlyOwner {}
    function unpause() public onlyOwner {}
    function setLawEnforcementRole(address _newLawEnforcementRole) public
{}
    modifier onlyLawEnforcementRole() {}
    function freeze(address _addr) public onlyLawEnforcementRole {}
    function unfreeze(address _addr) public onlyLawEnforcementRole {}
    function wipeFrozenAddress(address _addr) public onlyLawEnforcementRole
{}
    function isFrozen(address _addr) public view returns (bool) {}
    function setSupplyController(address _newSupplyController) public {}
    modifier onlySupplyController() {}
    function increaseSupply(uint256 _value) public onlySupplyController
returns (bool success) {}
    function decreaseSupply(uint256 _value) public onlySupplyController
returns (bool success) {}
}
```

`PaxImplementaion` contains several core functionalities. Here is a high-level overview of these functionalities:

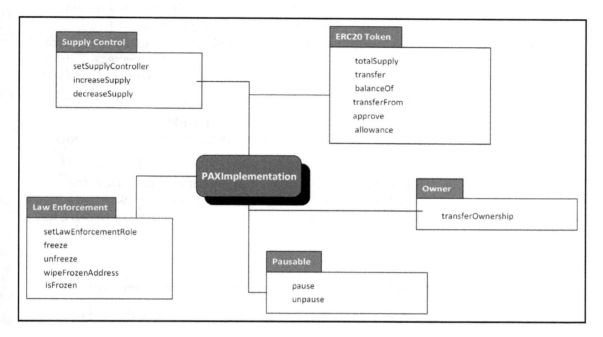

The contract implements five functionalities:

- **ERC20 Token**: Pax implements an ERC-20 interface to make it a standard ERC-20 token. The token can use all Ethereum wallets.
- **Owner**: It allows the current owner to transfer ownership by calling `transferOwnership()`.
- **Pausable**: It allows the contract owner to pause and unpause transfers and receive tokens in the contract in case of an emergency case, for example, a contract upgrade, a serious bug, and so on.

- **Law Enforcement**: It allows a user who's been assigned a **Law Enforcement** role to freeze/unfreeze addresses and seize their tokens. It checks whether the specific address is **isFrozen**. **wipeFrozenAddress** can wipe the balance of a frozen address, hence burning the tokens and setting the approval to zero.
- **Supply Control**: This functionality allows you to burn/mint tokens to control supply. It can increase supply by calling **increaseSupply** and decrease supply by calling **decreaseSupply**. Only `SupplyController` or the **Owner** can perform supply control functions.

The Paxos standard is easy to use, and the code is available on GitHub. To better understand Paxos design, you can run the Paxos smart contract test locally to see how it works.

You can simply `git clone` to your local environment. If you run the code from the previous chapter, `Chapter 6`, *Building a Security Token Dapp*, the security token `MyERC1404` example, you should have set up your local environment. Follow these steps to run a test for Paxos contracts:

1. Download the source code from GitHub:

   ```
   git clone https://github.com/paxosglobal/pax-contracts.git
   ```

2. Navigate to the project folder and run `npm install` to install the node dependency.
3. Then, run the `truffle test` command. You will see the Paxos smart contract test run. There should be around `83` test cases. The test result will be as follows:

```
  sub
    √ subtracts correctly (46ms)
    √ throws an error if subtraction result would be negative (47ms)

Contract: PAX
  as a supply-controlled token
    after token creation
      √ sender should be token owner (38ms)
      √ sender should be supply controller (41ms)
      √ total supply should be zero (45ms)
      √ balances should be zero (70ms)
    increaseSupply
      √ reverts when sender is not supply controller (57ms)
      √ adds the requested amount (121ms)
      √ emits a SupplyIncreased and a Transfer event (73ms)
      √ cannot increaseSupply resulting in positive overflow of the totalSupply (282ms)
    decreaseSupply
      when the supply controller has insufficient tokens
        √ reverts (57ms)
      when the supply controller has sufficient tokens
        √ reverts when sender is not supply controller (47ms)
        √ removes the requested amount (133ms)
        √ emits a SupplyDecreased and a Transfer event (70ms)
    setSupplyController
      √ reverts if sender is not owner or supplyController (49ms)
      √ works if sender is supply controller (105ms)
      √ reverts if newSupplyController is address zero (50ms)
      √ enables new supply controller to increase and decrease supply (405ms)
      √ prevents old supply controller from increasing and decreasing supply (92ms)
      √ emits a SupplyControllerSet event

Contract: Pausable PAX
  √ can transfer in non-pause (143ms)
  √ cannot transfer in pause (166ms)
  √ cannot approve/transferFrom in pause (247ms)
  √ should resume allowing normal process after pause is over (247ms)
  √ cannot unpause when unpaused or pause when paused (169ms)

83 passing (1m)
```

Let's take a look at GUSD.

GUSD

Gemini has launched its own stablecoin named GUSD. Similar to the Paxos standard, it is a regulated stablecoin. The token is under the supervision of the NYSDFS and is required to comply with the New York Banking Law.

GUSD is an ERC-20 compliant token. GUSD contracts are composed of a set of cooperating contracts. Here is a high-level smart contract diagram for GUSD:

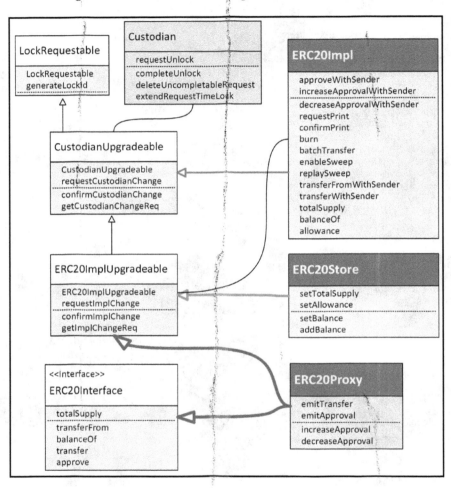

There are three cooperating contracts: **ERC20Proxy**, **ERC20Impl**, and **ERC20Store**.

ERC20Proxy

This contract implements `ERC20Interface` and extends from `ERC20ImplUpgradable`. The user only needs to interact with the `ERC20Proxy` smart contract. This proxy interface is the permanent interface to the GUSD. The contract proxy implementation is upgradable and can be changed from time to time.

The `Proxy` class wraps all of the implementation from `ERC20Impl`. For example, `decreaseApproval` calls the `ERC20Impl.decreaseApprovalWithSender` function:

```
function decreaseApproval(address _spender, uint256 _subtractedValue)
public returns (bool success) {
        return erc20Impl.decreaseApprovalWithSender(msg.sender, _spender,
_subtractedValue);
    }
```

The `decreaseApproval` and `increaseApproval` functions are used to handle the permitted spender amount:

- `decreaseApproval`: Decreases the permitted spender amount that can be withdrawn from your account
- `increaseApproval`: Increases the permitted spender amount that can be withdrawn from your account

ERC20Impl

This contract encapsulates all of the logic of the GUSD token. `ERC20Proxy` extends `ERC20ImplUpgradable`, and `ERC20ImplUpgradable` is associated with `ERC20Impl`. `_ERC20Proxy_` delegates the execution of ERC-20 functions to its trusted instance, `ERC20Impl`.

The following functions are defined and implemented in `ERC20Impl`:

```
contract ERC20Impl is CustodianUpgradeable {
...
    CustodianUpgradeable(_custodian) public {}
    function approveWithSender(address _sender, address _spender, uint256
_value
    ) public onlyProxy returns (bool success){}
    function increaseApprovalWithSender(address _sender, address _spender,
uint256 _addedValue) public onlyProxy returns (bool success) {}
    function decreaseApprovalWithSender(address _sender, address _spender,
uint256 _subtractedValue) public onlyProxy returns (bool success){}
    function requestPrint(address _receiver, uint256 _value) public returns
(bytes32 lockId) {}
    function confirmPrint(bytes32 _lockId) public onlyCustodian {}
    function burn(uint256 _value) public returns (bool success) {}
    function batchTransfer(address[] _tos, uint256[] _values) public
returns (bool success) {}
    function enableSweep(uint8[] _vs, bytes32[] _rs, bytes32[] _ss, address
_to) public onlySweeper {}
```

```
    function replaySweep(address[] _froms, address _to) public onlySweeper
{}
    function transferFromWithSender(address _sender, address _from, address
_to, uint256 _value) public onlyProxy returns (bool success) {}
    function transferWithSender(address _sender, address _to, uint256
_value)
        public onlyProxy returns (bool success) {}
    function totalSupply() public view returns (uint256) {}
    function balanceOf(address _owner) public view returns (uint256
balance) {}
    function allowance(address _owner, address _spender) public view
returns (uint256 remaining) {}

}
```

Let's take a look at these functions:

- requestPrint(): This sends a request to increase the token supply. Moreover, the newly created tokens will be added to the balance of the receiver account.
- confirmPrint(): This confirms a pending increase in the token supply.
- burn: This burns a certain amount of tokens from the sender's balance.
- batchTransfer(): This enables a sender to batch transfer multiple different addresses at once.
- enableSweep(): By signing the value of sweepMsg, you can delegate transfer control to the sweeper account. It also transfers the balances when enabling delegation.
- replaySweep(): The sweeper account can transfer some address balances to the given destination. The transaction transfer gas is quite efficient.

ERC20Store

This contract serves as the storage of the GUSD in Ethereum blockchain:

- setTotalSupply(): This sets the total supply of tokens
- setAllowance(): This sets the allowance that the owner is allowed to spend and transfer
- setBalance(): This sets the owner address balance

- addBalance(): This adds the new amount of balance to the owner account
- ERC20ImplUpgradeable: This contract extends from CustodianUpgradeable and provides reusable code for upgradeable implementations:

```
function generateLockId() internal returns (bytes32 lockId) {
    return keccak256(block.blockhash(block.number - 1), address(this),
++lockRequestCount);
    }
```

- LockRequestable(): This contract generates unique identifiers:
    - CustodianUpgradeable: This contract extends from LockRequestable. It provides a function to upgrade custodianship.
    - requestCustodianChange(): This sends a request to change the custodian.
    - confirmCustodianChange: This confirms a pending custodian change request.
    - Custodian: This contract provides dual control for cooperating contracts through a callback mechanism.
    - requestUnlock(): This sends requests to unlock a lock identifier. The lock identifier needs to be in a whitelisted address.
    - completeUnlock(): The function needs two signatures to complete a pending unlocking.
    - deleteUncompletableRequest(): If a pending request sharing the callback of a later request has been completed, this request becomes uncompletable and this function will reclaim the storage of the uncompletable request.
    - extendRequestTimeLock(): This extends the time lock of a pending request.

JPM Coin

JP Morgan announces a stablecoin, JPM Coin, in the quorum blockchain platform on February 2019. JPM Coin is still not an official release; it is in its prototype stages. The aim of JPM Coin is to be able to run on all standard blockchain networks. The JPM Coin is designed to support USD and other currencies. It has a value ratio of 1:1 to USD.

Its payment flow is considered traditional and has at least four transactions across interbank networks through a central bank. This centralized design for a payment clearing system is inefficient and slow. JPM Coin provides **real-time gross settlement** (**RTGS**) to clear and settle payments.

There are three steps in the process flow:

1. The client deposits USD and receives the same amount of JPM Coin
2. The client uses JPM Coin to perform a transaction with another JPM client in the blockchain network (for example, money movement and payments in securities transactions)
3. The client redeems their USD by using the equivalent number of JPM Coins in the network

The following diagram shows how it works:

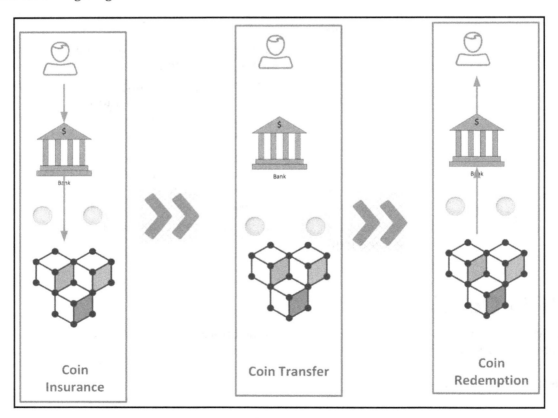

The preceding diagram depicts the three steps in the process flow: **Coin Insurance**, **Coin Transfer**, and **Coin Redemption**.

Summary

In this chapter, we reviewed the basic features of popular stablecoin and understood the three types of stablecoin, including fiat collateralized stablecoins, crypto collateralized stablecoins, and non-collateralized stablecoins.

Then, we looked into USDT, DAI, TUSD, USDC, GUSD, and PAX stablecoin smart contract design and explored the functions that are defined in these contracts. We learned how each stablecoin system maintains stable tokens with a 1:1 price peg through mint, burn, and other controllable functions.

Other Books You May Enjoy

If you enjoyed this book, you may be interested in these other books by Packt:

Blockchain Quick Start Guide
Xun (Brian) Wu, Weimin Sun

ISBN: 978-1-78980-797-4

- Understand how blockchain hashing works
- Write and test a smart contract using Solidity
- Develop and test a decentralized application
- Build and test your application using Hyperledger Fabric
- Implement business network using Hyperledger Composer
- Test and interact with business network applications

Mastering Blockchain - Second Edition
Imran Bashir

ISBN: 978-1-78883-904-4

- Master the theoretical and technical foundations of the blockchain technology
- Understand the concept of decentralization, its impact, and its relationship with blockchain technology
- Master how cryptography is used to secure data - with practical examples
- Grasp the inner workings of blockchain and the mechanisms behind bitcoin and alternative cryptocurrencies
- Understand the theoretical foundations of smart contracts
- Learn how Ethereum blockchain works and how to develop decentralized applications using Solidity and relevant development frameworks
- Identify and examine applications of the blockchain technology - beyond currencies
- Investigate alternative blockchain solutions including Hyperledger, Corda, and many more
- Explore research topics and the future scope of blockchain technology

Leave a review - let other readers know what you think

Please share your thoughts on this book with others by leaving a review on the site that you bought it from. If you purchased the book from Amazon, please leave us an honest review on this book's Amazon page. This is vital so that other potential readers can see and use your unbiased opinion to make purchasing decisions, we can understand what our customers think about our products, and our authors can see your feedback on the title that they have worked with Packt to create. It will only take a few minutes of your time, but is valuable to other potential customers, our authors, and Packt. Thank you!

Index

1

12-blocks-in-depth 26

A

absolute value of money 97
adjustable peg 105
AirFox case
  facts 77
  legal analysis, SEC 78
Alternative Trading System (ATS) 53
Anti-Money Laundering (AML) 46
arbitrage 97

B

B-money 20
bad actor disqualification 61
Bank Secrecy Act (BSA) 49
bartering 90
base money 93
Basecoin 107
bitcoin
  about 8, 100
  basics 14
  consensus mechanism 16
  digital wallets 18
  distributed ledger 15
  immutability feature 9
  keys 18, 19
  transparency feature 9
bitUSD 102
blockchain industry 9
blockchain technology
  bitcoin 8
  Ethereum 10
  evolution 12
  overview 8

Blockchain
  evolution, generation 13
  securities laws development 68
BTS 102

C

Casper 27
centralized stablecoins 107
Chai 144
chaincode 12
characteristics, money
  about 93
  divisibility 95
  durability 94
  general acceptability 96
  limited supply 96
  portability 94
  uniformity 95
client-side code 13
CoinMarketCap
  reference 56
collateralization 105
Collateralized Debt Position (CDP) 106
commercial bank money 93
Commodity Futures Trading Commission (CFTC)
  48
commodity money
  versus fiat currency 97
commodity peg 105
commodity-collateralized stablecoins 105
consensus mechanism 16, 17, 18
Consumer Price Index (CPI) 103
crawling peg 105
credit money 93
crowdfunding
  Equity crowdfunding 40
  Rewards crowdfunding 40

Crypto Asset Management case
  about 83
  legal analysis, by SEC 84
crypto collateralized stablecoins 102, 106, 186
cryptocurrencies 89

D

Dai 184
DAO report
  facts 71
  legal analysis, by SEC 72
  SEC's conclusion 74
  security trading 74
Dapp web components
  boilerplates code, cleaning 166
  ERC1404 UI components, implementing 170
  HTML template, defining 168
  project, setting up 163
  writing 162
Dapps (decentralized applications) 13
Decentralized Autonomous Organization (DAO) 39
decentralized stablecoins 107
Department of Justice (DOJ) 67
determinism 24
digital cryptocurrencies 68
digital wallets 18, 19
Digix Gold Tokens (DGX) 102
distributed ledger 9, 15, 16
distributed ledger technology (DLT) 13
DS apps 126
DS service 126
DS-Token (Securitize)
  about 125
  ownership architecture 125, 128

E

EduCoin 41
elliptic curve digital signature algorithm (ECDSA)
  24
enterprise blockchain 11
ERC-1404 token 128, 130
ERC-20 token 111, 112
ERC-721 token
  about 111
  NFTs 114, 115

ERC-884 token 130, 133
ERC1404 UI components
  accounts, loading 170
  AddAddressToWhitelist UI component 177
  DetectTransferRestriction UI component 175
  implementing 170
  MessageForTransferRestriction UI component
    176
  transfer UI component, implementing 172
  verifyWhitelist UI component 179
Ethereum development environment
  setting up 146
Ethereum gas 22
Ethereum Improvement Proposal (EIP) 116
Ethereum Request for Comment (ERC) 20, 112
Ethereum virtual machine (EVM) 10, 138
Ethereum
  about 28
  account, types 23
  basics 19
  components 27
  cryptocurrency 20
  off-the-chain data, scenarios 25
  performance considerations 26
  Proof of Stake (PoS) 26
  smart contract 21
  tokens 20
  virtual machine 22
European Securities and Markets Authority
  (ESMA) 47

F

federal regulations, Blockchain space
  about 57
  regulators 66
  section 3(a)(11) / Rule 147 (added by JOBS Act
    2012) 63
  section 3(b)(1) and (2) / Regulation A/A+
    offerings (Mini IPOs) 58
  Section 3(b)(1)/ Rule 504 – small issuance 60
  Section 4(a)(2) / Reg D– Rule 506(b) and (c) –
    private placement exemption 59
  section 4(a)(5) – accredited investor exemption
    62
  section 4(a)(6) / Regulation Crowdfunding 62

Securities Act of 1933, section 5 57
fiat collateralized stablecoins 186
fiat currency
  example, USD 99
fiat-collateralized stablecoins 106
Financial Conduct Authority (FCA) 47
Financial Crimes Enforcement Network (FinCEN) 66
Financial Industry Regulatory Authority (FINRA) 61
Finney 20
foreclosure 105
fork 16
fractional reserve banking 93
fungibility 95
fungible token (FT) 113

G

Ganache
  about 144
  features 144
  security tokens, deploying to 150
Gemini dollar (GUSD)
  about 102, 184, 185, 203
  ERC20Impl 205
  ERC20Proxy 204
  ERC20Store 206
genesis block 9
Gold Standard Act 99

H

hard fork 16
hardware oracles 25
Howey test 71, 72
Hyperledger Burrow 12
Hyperledger Fabric (HF) 11, 12
Hyperledger Indy 12
Hyperledger Iroha 12
Hyperledger Sawtooth 12

I

I owe you (IOU) 186
inflation problem 98
initial coin offering (ICO)
  about 29, 37, 41, 43, 46, 47
  coins 38

crowdfunding 40
reference 43
tokens 38
versus IPO 41
Initial Public Offering (IPO)
  about 29, 35, 55
  cons 36
  pros 36
Internal Revenue Service (IRS) 48
intrastate offering
  about 63
  regulatory issues 63
  securities, limited offerings 59
intrinsic value of money 97
investment contract 72, 73

J

Java Virtual Machine (JVM) 22
JPM Coin 100, 207
Jumpstart Our Business Startups Act (JOBS Act) 58

K

keys 18
Know Your Customer (KYC) 46
know your customer (KYC)/anti-money laundering (AML) verification 113
Kohlberg Kravis Roberts (KKR) 34

L

Linux Foundation (LF) 11
Lisp Like Language (LLL) 10

M

Membership Service Provider (MSP) 12
Mini IPO 58
minimal reserve amount 93
mining 16
mining rig 16
Mocha 144
Money Laundering Control Act (MLCA) 49
money multiplier effect 93
money
  absolute value 97

basics 90
characteristics 93
commercial bank money 93
commodity money 92
durability 94
evolution, historical events 90
fiat currency 92
fiduciary money 93
relative value 97
multiplier factor 93
Munchee Inc. (Munchee order)
facts 75
legal analysis, by SEC 76
Mutan 22

N

National Security Agency (NSA) 100
New York State Department of Financial Services
(NYSDFS) 67, 184
New York Stock Exchange (NYSE) 43
node 14
non-collateralized stablecoins 107, 187
non-fungible token (NFT) 113

O

object-oriented programming (OOP)
abstract 140
Offering Circular (OC) 58
Omni Wallet 188
opcod 22
Oracle 24
orderer nodes 12
over-the-counter (OTC) 11

P

P2P transfer And Storage 188
Paragon case
about 79
legal analysis, SEC 80
Paxos Standard (PAX) 102, 184, 185, 199, 202
peg
about 104
adjustable peg 105
basket peg 105
crawling peg 105

Plasma 27
Polymath
exchange transfer manager module 121
transfer manager module 121
Pooled Ether (PETH) 196
primary functions, money
about 91
medium of exchange 91
unit of account 91
primary stablecoin
overview 183
private blockchain 11
Private Equity (PE) 29
Proof of Elapsed Time (PoET) 12
Proof of Stake (PoS) 26
proof of work (PoW) 16, 100
public blockchain 11
purchasing power 97
Purchasing Power Parity (PPP) 98

Q

Qualified Institutional Buyers (QIBs) 68

R

randomization methods
coin age-based selection 26
delegated PoS 26
randomized block selection 26
randomized PoS 26
real cases, of federal securities law violation
about 74
AirFox case 77
Crypto Asset Management case 83
Munchee Inc. (Munchee order), facts 75
Paragon case 79
SEC versus PlexCorps et al 82
TokenLot LLC case 85
real-time gross settlement (RTGS) 208
registered investment advisor 66
registered transfer agent (RTA) 133
Regulation A+
tier-1 offer requirements 58
tier-2 offer requirements 59
Regulation Crowdfunding (Reg CF) 40
regulatory regimes

Investment Advisor Act of 1940 66
issuers—Investment Company Act of 1940 65
securities trading platform 65
security fraud Rule 10b-5 64
regulatory risk
  about 50
  examples 50
relative value of money 97
resale of securities Rule 144/144A/Section 4(a)(1½
) / Section 4(a)(7)
  about 67
  rule 144 exemption 67
  rule 144A exemption 68
  section 4(a)(1½) exemption 68
  section 4(a)(7) exemption 68
reusable proofs of work (RPOW) 20
Ripple (XRP) 100
Rule 504
  limitations 61
Rule 506
  limitations 61

S

Sawtooth 12
secondary functions, money
  standard of deferred payments 92
  store of value 92
  transfer of money 92
Securities and Exchange Commission (SEC)
  about 32
  alerts 69
  versus PlexCorps et al 82
securities laws development
  report of Investigation Pursuant 71
securitization 8
security token offerings (STO)
  about 7, 47, 49, 55, 56
  challenges 52, 53
  launch and legal considerations 86
  reference 47
  security 48
  verses ICO 49
  versus IPO 50, 52
security token smart contract
  creating 152

deploying 152
detectTransferRestriction, implementing 154
implementing 153
information, defining 153
messageForTransferRestriction, implementing
  155
test case, initializing 156, 162
test case, setting up 156, 162
testing 152, 156
transfer, implementing 155
transferFrom, implementing 155
security token Truffle project
  creating 148
  deploying, to Ganache 150
seigniorage shares approach 107
Serpent 22
sharding approach 27
smart contracts
  about 21, 133
  abstract 140
  comments 135
  enum 139
  events 138
  function modifiers 138
  functions 137
  import 135
  inheritance 140
  interface 140
  paths 136
  Pragma keyword 134
  state variables 137
  struct 139
social and institutional durability 94
soft fork 16
software oracle 25
ST-20 (security token standard)
  about 119
  module 121
  Module Factory 121
  polymath registries 121
  ST version proxy 121
stablecoin
  about 102
  advantages 103
  basics 99

challenges 108
ciat-collateralized stablecoins 106
commodity peg 105
commodity-collateralized stablecoins 105
crypto collateralized stablecoins 186
cryptocurrency 100
development, timeline 184
fiat collateralized stablecoins 186
fiat-collateralized stablecoins 106
non-collateralized stablecoins 107, 187
stability, testing 103
technical design, overview 188
types 104, 185
state regulations
    about 67
    resale of securities Rule 144/144A/Section
        4(a)(1½) / Section 4(a)(7) 67
STO smart contract development tools
    about 143
    Ganache 144
    Truffle 144

T

technical design, stablecoin
    GUSD 203
    Paxos Standard (PAX) 199
    tether (USDT) 188, 189
    token-related contracts 195
    TrueUSD (TUSD) smart contract 191
    USD coin (USDC) 197
Tether 184
tether (USDT)
    Bitcoin Blockchain 188
    Omni layer protocol 188
throughput per second (TPS) 27
token technical design, security
    DS-Token (Securitize) 125
    ERC-1400/ERC-1410 116, 118
    overview 116
    R-Token 122, 123
    SRC-20 124

ST-20 (security token standard) 119
token-related contracts
    MakerDAO (Dai) 195
TokenLot LLC case
    about 85
    legal analysis, by SEC 86
traditional fund raising roadmap, for startups
    about 30
    angel funds 31
    angel investors 31
    IPO 35
    mezzanine capital/fund 34
    private equity firms 33
    seed money 31
    stages 30
    VC fund 32
Truebit 27
TrueUSD (TUSD) smart contract
    about 191
    admin 193
    modularERC20 192
    proxy 192
    token-related contracts 193
Truffle 144
TUSD 184

U

Uniform Regulation of Virtual Currency Business
    Act (URVCBA) 67
US Dollar Index (USDX) 104
US securities laws
    overview 57
USD coin (USDC) 184, 197, 198
use value 97

V

Venture Capital (VC) 29

X

xRapid 100

www.ingramcontent.com/pod-product-compliance
Lightning Source LLC
Chambersburg PA
CBHW080523060326
40690CB00022B/5005